The *South Beach* method for Conversational German

By: Erasmus-Cromwell Smith

ISBN: 979-8-9866136-3-5

Publisher: Erasmus Press
Editor and Proofreading: Elisa Arraiz Lucca
Cover Design and Interior Design: Abjini Shamanik
www.erasmuscromwellsmith.com

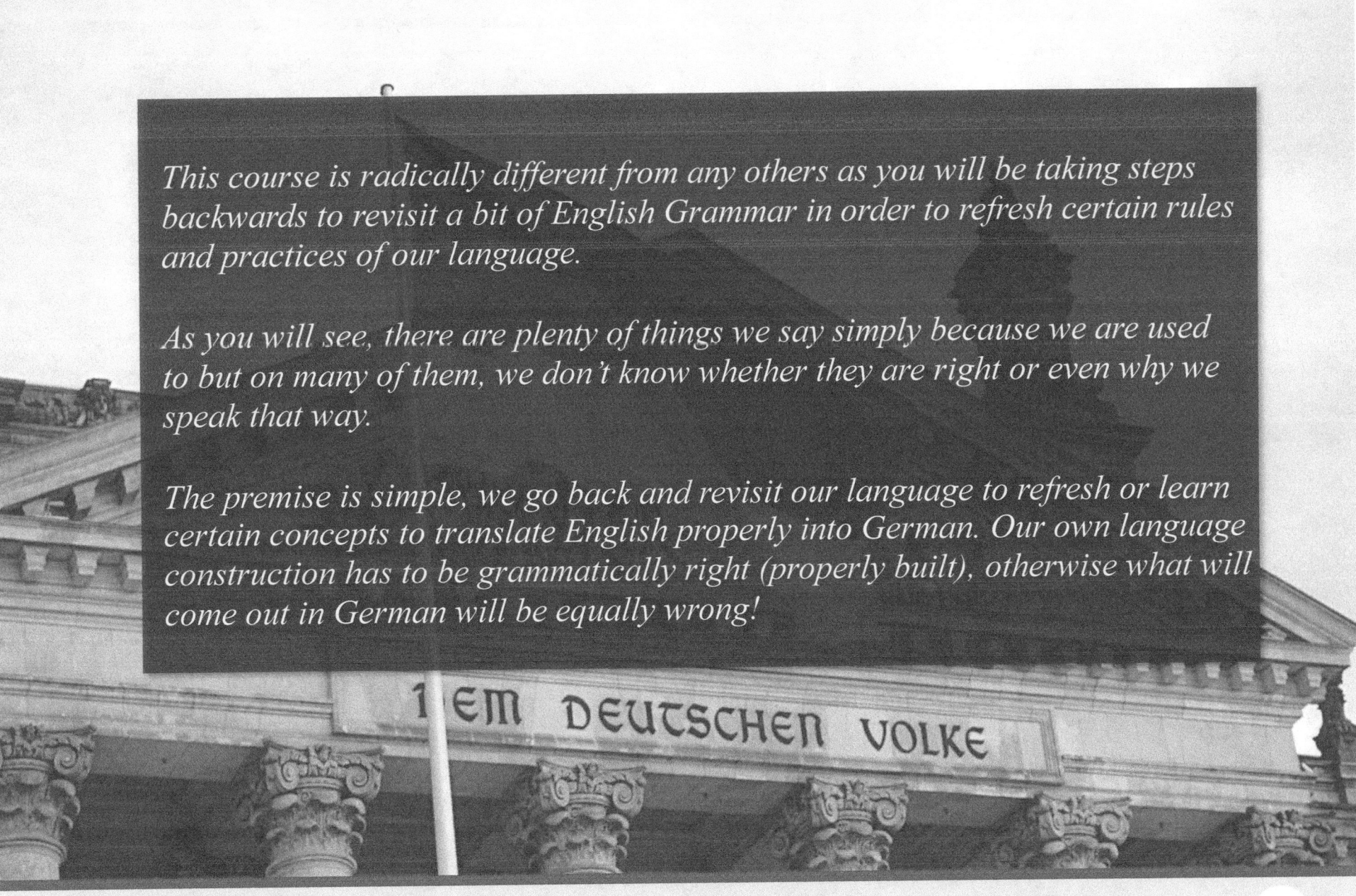

This course is radically different from any others as you will be taking steps backwards to revisit a bit of English Grammar in order to refresh certain rules and practices of our language.

As you will see, there are plenty of things we say simply because we are used to but on many of them, we don't know whether they are right or even why we speak that way.

The premise is simple, we go back and revisit our language to refresh or learn certain concepts to translate English properly into German. Our own language construction has to be grammatically right (properly built), otherwise what will come out in German will be equally wrong!

Conversational German

➢ This course will enable you to speak German within hours.

➢ This course debunks the idea that German is a very hard language to learn.

➢ Actually, in most cases, both languages are spoken in the same way (literally like a mirror image).

➢ The Foundation of this method is the Infinitive Verbs.

➢ You will learn to speak through 4 templates (all of them using Infinitive Verbs).

➢ The method also teaches you how to pronounce/spell properly in German.

➢ It also allows/enables you to study/learn most German Verbs only in Infinitive Form (almost without conjugations) effectively cutting thousands of hours and thousands of verb conjugations from the learning process.

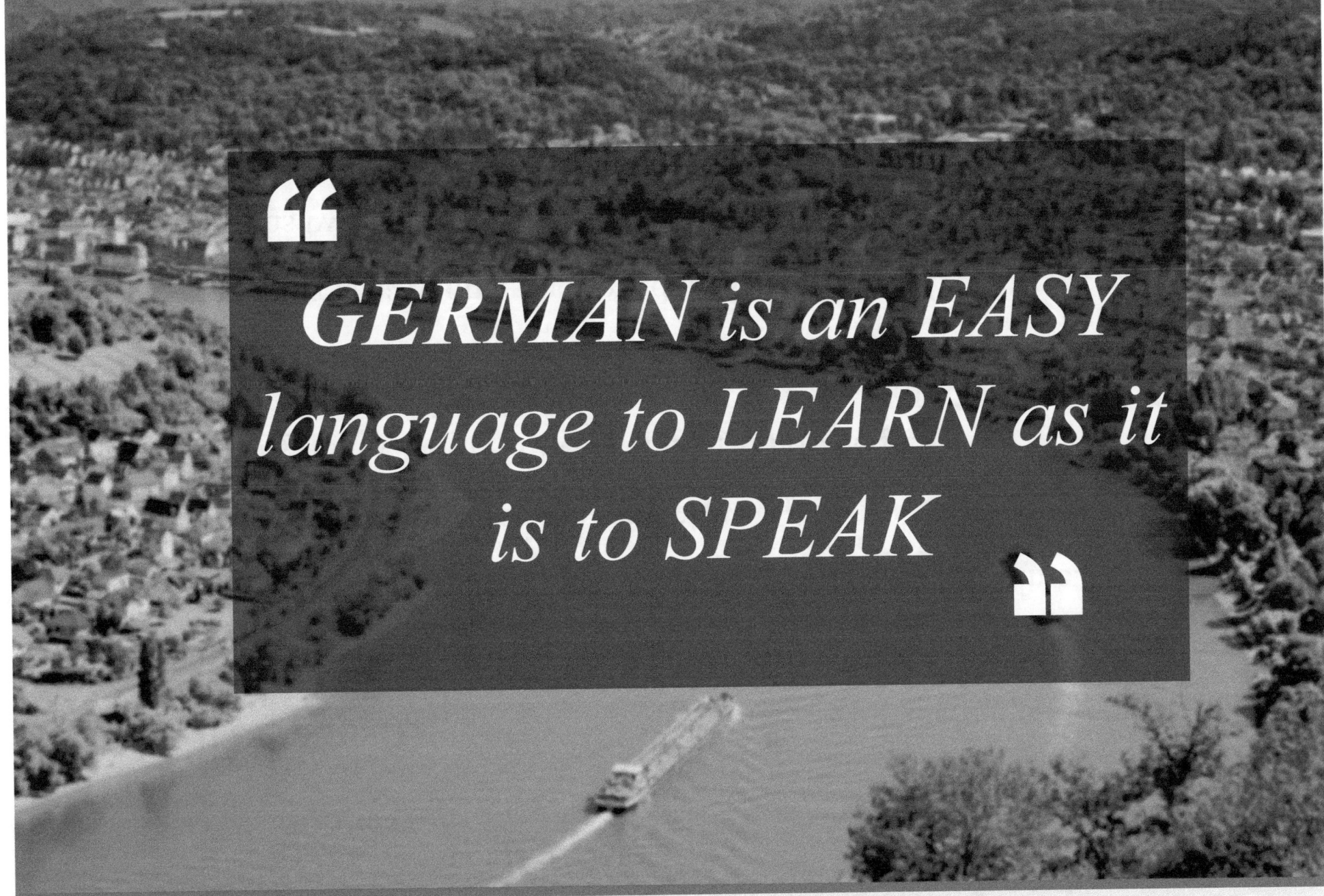

"GERMAN is an EASY language to LEARN as it is to SPEAK"

Let Us Begin...

For the most part:

> ➢ German is spoken the same way English is!

> ➢ Most of the grammar rules (even their names) are the same.

> ➢ Phrases are structured the same way.

> ➢ Many, many words are very similar if not the same.

German difficulty debunked:

German vowels have only one sound: **AH-EH-E-OH-OOH**

English has two or more sounds per vowel!

So, let's debunk the idea that German is so difficult!

Learning Step 1

Everything Begins With

The 5 Vowels

Next you will learn how to pronounce them easily!

The Basics First: "The Vowels"

german Vowel	German Pronunciation			Easy: Pronunciation is in parenthesis ( )		
A (AH) Read Aloud	Ah Again	Ah Again	Ah Again	Ah Again	Ah
E (EH)	EH	EH	EH	EH	EH
I (E)	E	E	E	E	E
O (OH)	OH	OH	OH	OH	OH
U (UH)	UH	UH	UH	UH	UH

Now let's practice them one after the other: AH-EH-E-OH-UH

Now do it faster: AH-EH-E-OH-UH now even faster: AH-EH-E-OH-UH

Keep on practicing : AH-EH-E-OH-UH ' until you memorize it .

AH-EH-E-OH-UH Repeat and memorize the sound.

AH-EH-E-OH-UH Try to do it faster & faster.

Learning Step 2

Next is to learn

The Alphabet

Pronunciation in German is in (parenthesis)!

Pronunciation and phonetics of the German Alphabet

A (ah)	B (beh)	C (tzeh)	D (deh)	E (eh)	F (ef)
G (geh)	H (hah)	I (e)	J (yot)	K (kah)	L (el)
M (em)	N (en)	O (oh)	P (peh)	Q (koo)	R (ehr)
S (s)	T (teh)	U (oo)	V (vau)	W (veh)	
X (iks)	Y (ypsilon)		Z (tzett)		

Learning Step 2

It is also very useful to learn

The Numbers

Eins	Zwei	Drei	Vier	Fünf	Sechs	Sieben	Acht	Neun
One	Two	Three	Four	Five	Six	Seven	Eight	Nine
Zehn	Zwanzig	Dreißig	Vierzig	Fünfzig	Sechzig	Siebzig	Achtzig	Neunzig
Ten	Twenty	Thirty	Forty	Fifty	Sixty	Seventy	Eighty	Ninety

(Ein)hundert	Zweihundert	Dreihundert	Vierhundert
One hundred	Two hundred	Three hundred	Four hundred
Fünfhundert	**Sechshundert**	**Siebenhundert**	**Achthundert**
Five hundred	Six hundred	Seven hundred	Eight hundred
Neunhundert	**(Ein)tausend**	**Zehntausend**	**(Ein)hunderttausend**
Nine hundred	One thousand	Ten thousand	One hundred thousand
Eine Million	**Einhundert Millionen**	**Eine Milliarde**	**Eine Billion**
One million	One hundred million	One billion	One trillion

Learning Step 3

Having learned the alphabet and the vowels, the next step is to learn:

The Nouns

Lesson 2: Part 1

I - You

Easy , just read it ! ()

Read it aloud		Read it aloud
I - Ich (Ich)	You – Du (do)	
Read it aloud		Read it aloud
I - Ich (Ich)	You – Du (do)	
Read it aloud		Read it aloud
I - Ich (Ich)	You – Du (do)	
Read it aloud		Read it aloud
I - Ich (Ich)	You – Du (do)	
Read it aloud		Read it aloud
I - Ich (Ich)	You – Du (do)	
Read it aloud		Read it aloud
I - Ich (Ich)	You – Du (do)	
Read it aloud		Read it aloud
I - Ich (Ich)	You – Du (do)	
Read it aloud		Read it aloud
I - Ich (Ich)	You – Du (do)	

*Remember in German I is **Ich**, You is **Du***

Lesson 2: Part 2

He - She

Easy , just read it ! ()

Read it aloud	Read it aloud
He – Er (air)	She – Sie (see)
He – Er (air)	She – Sie (see)
He – Er (air)	She – Sie (see)
He – Er (air)	She – Sie (see)
He – Er (air)	She – Sie (see)
He – Er (air)	She – Sie (see)
He – Er (air)	She – Sie (see)
He – Er (air)	She – Sie (see)

*Remember in German He is **Er**, She is **Sie***

Lesson 2: Part 3

We - You	Easy , just read it ! ()
Read it aloud	Read it aloud
We – Wir (we're)	You – Ihr (ear)
Read it aloud	Read it aloud
We – Wir (we're)	You – Ihr (ear)
Read it aloud	Read it aloud
We – Wir (we're)	You – Ihr (ear)
Read it aloud	Read it aloud
We – Wir (we're)	You – Ihr (ear)
Read it aloud	Read it aloud
We – Wir (we're)	You – Ihr (ear)
Read it aloud	Read it aloud
We – Wir (we're)	You – Ihr (ear)
Read it aloud	Read it aloud
We – Wir (we're)	You – Ihr (ear)
Read it aloud	Read it aloud
We – Wir (we're)	You – Ihr (ear)

*Remember in German <u>We</u> is **Wir**, <u>You</u> is **Sie***

They - It

Easy , just read it ! ()

Read it aloud	Read it aloud
They - Sie (see)	It – Es (s)
Read it aloud	Read it aloud
They - Sie (see)	It – Es (s)
Read it aloud	Read it aloud
They - Sie (see)	It – Es (s)
Read it aloud	Read it aloud
They - Sie (see)	It – Es (s)
Read it aloud	Read it aloud
They - Sie (see)	It – Es (s)
Read it aloud	Read it aloud
They - Sie (see)	It – Es (s)
Read it aloud	Read it aloud
They - Sie (see)	It – Es (s)
Read it aloud	Read it aloud
They - Sie (see)	It – Es (s)

*Remember in German They is **Sie**, It is **Es***

Lesson 2

SUMMARY	The Nouns		Easy, just read it! ()
Let's continue to practice!	I - Ich	(Ich)	Repeat it 5 times!
	You - Du	(do)	Repeat it 5 times!
	He - Er	(air)	Repeat 5 more times
	She - Sie	(see)	This one 5 times as well
	We - Wir	(we're)	Pronounce this one 5 times
	You - Ihr	(ear)	This one 5 times as well
	They - Sie	(see)	5 times with this as well
	It - Es	(s)	This one 5 times as well

The following are essential to any conversation:

Magic Words

Practice them!

Lesson 3: Part 1

Let us introduce a few words that are essential in any conversation

Ein/Eine Einer/Eines	=	ein einer / eine eines / einer	Yes No	= Ja = Nein	
The	=	Der Die Das	At	= Bei/beim	
And	=	und	To	= zu	
With	=	mit	That	= dass	
Or	=	oder	This	= das/dies	

Lesson 3: Part 2

What	=	was	But	=	aber
When	=	wann, ob	Whose	=	wessen
Where	=	wo	Who	=	wer
Why/Because	=	warum/weil	Which	=	welches
Whether	=	ob	How	=	wie
To	=	zu	For	=	für, zum
From	=	von	While	=	während
How Many	=	Wie viel(e)	Whom	=	wem, wessen
For	=	für, zum	As	=	als
More than	=	Mehr als	How Much	=	Wie viel

A

A: ein, eine, einer, eines
About To: gerade dabei
Against: gegen
Although: Obwohl
And: und
As…As: so…wie
At (place): bei/beim
At What Time: Zu welcher Zeit
A Little: Ein wenig
Above: über
Ago: vor
Already: schon, bereits
And Now, What: Und was jetzt
As Long As: solange
At (hour): um (time)
Awful: grässlich
A Little Bit: etwas, ein wenig
After: nach
All: alles
Also: so, auch
Another: ein anderes

As Soon As: sobald
At this Moment: in diesem Moment

A Lot: viel
Afterwards: danach
All Day: den ganzen Tag
Always: immer
Anybody: jeder
About: über
Again: wieder
Almost: fast
Amusing: amüsant
As: als, wie
Appointed: verabredet
At This Time: um diese Zeit

B

Barely: fast
Between: zwischen
Butter: Butter
Because: weil
Bit: bisschen

By: von, durch
Before: bevor
Both: beide
By The Way: übrigens
Behind: hinter
Breakdown: Zusammenbruch
Below: unter
But: aber

C

Careful: vorsichtig
Caution: Vorsicht
Certain: bestimmte
Careful: vorsichtig
Caution: Vorsicht
Certain: bestimmte

D

Dear: Liebe/r
Difficult: schwer
Departure: Abreise
Despite: trotz

Lesson 3: Part 2

Detour: Umleitung
Divided By: geteilt durch

F
Fair: Messe, Expo
Fine: Strafe
Further: weiter
Far: weit
For: für
Fault: Schuld
For The Reason: weil, wegen
Feasible: bezahlbar
Few: wenig
From: von

G
Generally: allgemein
Good: gut

H
Half: halb

How Long: wie lange
Heavy: schwer
How Much: wie viel
How: wie
Hot: heiß

I
If: wenn
Impossible: unmöglich
In front of: vor
In good health: gesund
Inside: innen, drinnen
It is necessary: Es ist notwendig
Immediately: sofort

Improbable: unwahrscheinlich
In case of: im Fall von
In order that: Für den Fall, das
Instead of: anstatt
It could be: es könnte sein
In: in

In case that: Im Fall, das
In order to: um
In spite of: Im Gegensatz
It maybe: es kann sein
Important: wichtig
In a hurry: in Eile
Included: Eingeschlossen
In the habit of: In der Gewohnheit
Interesting: interesant

J
Just: nur

K
Keep: sorgen
Kind: nett

L
Lacking: fehlt

Latest: neuste
Least: zuletzt

Likely: wahrscheinlich
List: Liste
Low: niedrig
Large: groß
Left: links
Little: klein, wenig
Last: neuste, neuster
Leftover: Reste
Long: lang
Late: spät
Looks Like: sieht aus wie
Later: später
Less: weniger
Late: spät
Looks Like: sieht aus wie
Later: später
Less: weniger

M
Made In: Hergestellt in
Mrs.: Frau

M
Made In: Hergestellt in
Mrs.: Frau
Many: viel
Much: viel
Maybe: vielleicht
Merely: gerade einmal
Miss.: Frau
More: mehr

N
Named (to be): benannt
Neither: nichts davon
Nothing: nichts
Narrow: eng
Never: nie, niemals
Now: jetzt
Near: nah, nahe
New: neu
Nearby: nahe
Next: nächste, weiter
Necessary: notwendig

Next to: neben
Not: nicht

O
Obvious: offensichtlich
On: auf, an
Open: offen, geöffnet
Outside: außen, draußen
Odd: ungerade, komisch
On Call: auf Abruf
Or: oder
Over: über, vorbei
Of: von
Once: einmal
Other: andere, anderer
Overcome: überstehen
Of course: natürlich
Ongoing: andauern
Otherwise: andernfalls
Overlook: überblicken
Often: oft

Only: nur
Out: aus

P
Percent: Prozent
Point: Punkt
Push: drücken
Perhaps: vielleicht
Probable: wahrscheinlich
Pleasant: angenehm
Problem: Problem
Perfectly: Perfekt
Program: Programm
Please: bitte
Pull: ziehen

Q
Question: Frage
Quite Enough: ausreichend

R
Ready: bereit, fertig

Repeat: wiederholen
Routine: Routine
Regularly: regelmäßig
Right Away: sofort, direkt
Responsible: verantwortlich
Right Now: sofort
Ridiculous: lächerlich
Relative: Angehöriger, Angehörige

S
See you Later: bis später
Sir: Herr
Something: etwas
Still: immernoch
Several: mehrere
So: Also
Somewhat: etwas
Stop: Stop
Show Me: zeig mir
Some: etwas, ein paar

So Much: so viel
Subject: Thema
Side: Seite
Somebody: Jemand
Soon: bald
Sure: sicher
Similar: ähnlich
Someone: jemand
Specific: spezifisch
Somewhere: irgendwo

T
Task: Aufgabe
The: der, die, das
Together: zusammen
Too (also): auch
There Will Be: es wird geben
That: das
There: da
Through: durch
Those: sie, diese
Therefore: daher

There: da
These: diese, dieser
To: für
Too Much: zu viel
There is/are: Es gibt
Thick: dick
Tomorrow: morgen
This Evening: heute Abend
There Have Been: es gab
This: dies, diese, dieser, dieses
Thing: Ding
Tonight: heute Abend
There was/were: es gab
There Would Be: es würde geben

U
Underneath: unter
Unlikely: unwahrscheinlich
Unwilling: nicht bereit
Under: unter
Up: oben
Until: bis
Useful: nützlich

Understood: verstanden
Unless: es sei denn
Unfortunately:
leider
Unpleasant: unangenehm

V
Very: sehr

W
Warm: warm
Why: warum
Where To: wohin
Without: ohne
With: mit
Whatever: wie auch immer
Whereby: wo in der Nähe
Whoever: wer auch immer
Watch Out: pass auf
Wide: weit, breit
Who: wer
With Me: mit mir
Whether: ob

Well: gut, nun
Which: welche, welcher, welches
With you: mit dir
Whole: komplett
Whereabouts:
Hinterlassenschaften
Wet Paint: nasse Farbe
What: was
When: wann
Where: wo
Whenever: wann immer
Which: welche, welcher, welches
With you: mit dir
Within: innerhalb
While: während
Who: wer
Whole komplett
Without: ohne
Whose: wessen
Y
Yet: schon
Yield: Ertrag

Learning Step 5

Reflexives and Possessives

are essential to complete a sentence

Practice them, emphasize the pronunciation

Reflexive / Reflexiv

German/English/Spelling   Examples

Ich (Ich)	Me	**Call me**	Ruf mich
Du (do)	You	**Bring you**	Bring dich
Ihm (Ihm)	Him	**Take him**	Nimm ihn
Ihr (ear)	Her	**Invite her**	Lade Sie ein
Unser (unser)	Us	**Get us**	Hole uns
Ihr (ear)	You	**Buy for you**	Kaufe für dich
Sie (see)	Them	**Write them**	Schreibe ihnen
Es (s)	It	**Sell it**	Verkaufe es

Possessive / Possessiv

Examples   German/English/Spelling

My home	Mein Zuhause	**Mein (mein)**	My
Your car	Dein Auto	**Dein (dein)**	Your
His son	Sein Sohn	**Sein (sein)**	His
Her pet	Ihr Haustier	**Ihr (ear)**	Her
Our boat	Unser Bot	**Unser (oonser)**	Our
Your dad	Dein Vater	**Euer (euer)**	Your
Their idea	Ihre Idee	**Ihr (ear)**	Their
Its tail	Sein Schwanz	**Su (Soo)**	Its

You	**have**	**to go**	**to take him**	**home**
Du	musst		ihn nach Hause bringen
You	**Have**	**to take**	**him**	**home**
Du	musst		ihn nach Hause bringen
He	**can**	**come**	**to see me**	**later**
Er	kann	später kommen	um mich zu sehen
They	**want**	**to bring**	**her to see**	**you**
Sie	wollen	sie bringen	damit du sie sehen kannst
They	**are**	**trying**	**to call**	**today**
Sie	versuchen		heute	anzurufen

You.	**are**	**welcome to**	**our**	**house**
Du	bist	in unserem haus	herzlich	willkommen
She	**is**	**driving**	**my**	**car**
Sie		fährt	mein	Auto
He	**has**	**to bring**	**my**	**son**
Er	muss	meinen Sohn		bringen
They	**want**	**to take**	**my**	**wife**
Sie	wollen	meine	Frau	nehmen
Today	**I want**	**to go**	**to my**	**studio**
Heute	will Ich	zu meinem	Studio	gehen

Lesson 3: Part 3

Notes on Reflexives: In German a reflexive can also be placed right after the noun (at the very beginning of the phrase), it is preferable this way.

Examples:
I will bring them home
Ich bringe sie nach hause
Ich werde sie nach hause bringen

I want to take him to the airport
Ich bringe ihn zum Flughafen
Ich werde ihn zum Flughafen bringen

I have to go to purchase the medicines for him
Ich gehe los um für ihn Medikamente zu kaufen
Ich werde für ihn Medikamente kaufen gehen

I can prepare food for you at twelve
Ich mache für dich um zwölf Essen
Ich werde um zwölf für dich Essen machen

Learning Step 6

The Infinitive Verbs

Are the foundation of this course they are used almost identically both in English and German

Practice them!

What is an Infinitive Verb?

1) Well, it starts with a "To" in English and ends with a "n" in German

    Example: <u>to</u> call   <u>to</u> come   <u>to</u> go   <u>to</u> eat

             anrufen   kommen   <u>gehen</u>   essen

2) It's never the 1st. verb (as it can't be conjugated)

    You can't say in English   I to call   I to come   I to go   I to eat

    You can't say in German   Ich gehen   Ich kommen   Ich werden Ich essen

3) But it's always used after the 2nd. Infinitive Verb. 2nd. and 3rd verbs are swapped.

    Example: I   want   to go   to eat

             Ich möchte essen gehen

             She wants   to come   to visit

             Sie möchte mich besuchen kommen

Lesson 4: Part 2

This course is built around the Infinitive Verbs

In English, infinitive verbs are used all the time:
I want to go to eat now.
He wants to come to visit you.

Germans use The Infinitive Verbs the same way. The 3rd and 5th words swapped!

All the time and in the same way we do !

I	want	to go	to eat	now
Ich	möchte	jetzt	essen	gehen
He	wants	to come	to visit	you
Er	möchte	dich	sehen	kommen

SMILE ☺ The only thing to do is to swap the order of the 3rd and 5th segments in the sentence.

This course is built around <u>the Infinitive Verbs</u>

Here are more examples!

I	have	to take	you	She	wants	to watch TV	'til midnight
Ich	muss	dich	bringen	Sie	will	Fersehen bis	Mitternacht gucken
You	**have**	**to bring**	**him**	**We**	**want**	**to go to shop**	**at noon**
Du	musst	ihn	bringen	Wir	möchten	mittags	shoppen gehen
He	**has**	**to go to see**	**you**	**They**	**want**	**to give you**	**a surprise**
Er	muss	dich	sehen	Sie	wollen	dir eine	Überraschung machen
We	**have**	**to try to get**	**there**	**You**	**want**	**to do him**	**a lot of good**
Wir	müssen	versuchen dort hinzukommen		Du	möchtest	ihm viel	Gutes tun

The 8 Phrases mirror each other word by word except that the 3rd and 4th segment are often exchanged. Instead of the word (to have) in English, that denotes duty and not possession, in German only the word **must** is used (müssen)

The two languages when spoken properly
Are spoken in the same way!

**All You Need To Be Conversant in German are <u>"The Infinitive Verbs"</u>
which are the Foundation of this method.**

- <u>The Infinitive Verbs</u> are used the same way and even on the same spot in both German and English .

- <u>The Infinitive Verbs</u> are never the 1st. Verb on a phrase:

<u>I   want   to have</u>
Ich möchte haben

- <u>The Infinitive Verbs</u> start with "To" in English:
And End with an m in German:

<u>To have</u>
haben

- <u>The Infinitive Verbs</u> cannot be conjugated:

I to have
Ich haben

- <u>The Infinitive Verbs</u> continue to be used on a phrase endlessly.
In this sense the 2 languages are identical

<u>I   want to go to eat</u>
Ich möchte essen gehen

- The 2nd. <u>Infinitive Verb</u> on a German Sentence
is always Preceded by an "A"

<u>I   want to go to sleep</u>
Ich möchte schlafen gehen

The <u>infinitive Verbs</u> enable through templates to be conversant in four tenses:
(1) Gerund-action, (2) Past Participle, (3) Future and (4) Conditional.

On the Next Page
You'll Find A
List Of,

Infinitive Verben
Infinitive Verbs

Study, Read and Spell them multiple times
'till they stick and……
Notice that all of them (well almost all)

Start with <u>To</u>   <u>in</u> English
End with <u>n</u>   in German

A

To Accept: akzeptieren
To Acquire: erhalten
To Allow: erlauben
To Announce: ankündigen
To Answer: antworten
To Argue: diskutieren
To Approve: bestätigen
To Arrive: ankommen
To Arrange: arrangieren
To Ask: fragen
To Assist: assistieren

B

To Be: sein
To Be: sein
To Be Angry: wütend sein
To Be Right: recht haben
To Be Thankful: dankbar sein
To Be Wrong: falsch liegen
To Become: werden
To Begin: beginnen, anfangen
To Believe: glauben
To Bring: bringen
To Build: bauen
To Buy: kaufen

C

To Cause: verursachen
To Call: rufen, anrufen
Can: können
To Clean: reinigen, säubern
To Close: schließen
To Collect: sammeln
To Come: kommen
To Complete: vervollständigen
To Cook: kochen
To Copy: kopieren
To Correct: korrigieren
Could: können
To Cry: weinen

D

To Dance: tanzen
To Depart: abreisen
To Discuss: diskutieren
To Do: tun
To Doubt: bezweifeln
To Dress: anziehen
To Drink: trinken
To Drive: fahren

E

To Earn: verdienen
To Eat: essen
To Enter: betreten
To Erase: löschen
To Exit: verlassen

F

To Fall: fallen
To Fear: fürchten
To Feel: fühlen
To Find: finden
To Find Out: herausfinden
To Finish: beenden
To Fit: passen
To Follow: folgen
To Forget: vergessen
To Forgive: vergeben

G

To Get: bekommen
To Get: erhalten
To Get: erreichen
To Get: werden
To Get: holen
To Give: geben
To Go: gehen
To Greet: grüßen
To Grow: wachsen

L

To Laugh: lachen
To Learn: lernen
To Leave: verlassen
To Lend: leihen
To Listen: zuhören
To Let; lassen
To Like: mögen
To Live: leben
To Look: gucken
To Look (like): aussehen
To Lose: verlieren
To Love: lieben
To Live: leben
To Look: gucken
To Look (like): aussehen
To Lose: verlieren
To Love: lieben

M

May: dürfen
To Make: machen
To Move: bewegen
Must: müssen

N

To Name: benennen
To Need: brauchen
To Nix: ablehnen
(Slang)

O

To Obey: unterwerfen
To Offer: anbieten
To Observe: beobachten
To Open: öffnen
To Order: bestellen
To Owe: schulden
To Own: besitzen

P

To Pardon: entschuldigen
To Pay: bezahlen
To Pick(select): auswählen
To Pick: wählen
To Play (instrument): spielen
To Pull: ziehen
To Purchase: kaufen
To Push: drücken
To Put: setzen

R

To Read: lesen
To Realize: realisieren
To Refuse: weigern
To Reject: ablehnen
To Remember: erinnern
To Repeat: wiederholen
To Reply: antworten
To Request: anfragen
To Respect: respektieren
To Rest: ausruhen
To Return: wiederkommen
To Run: rennen

S

To Save: aufbewahren
To Satisfy: zufriedenstellen
To Say: sagen
To See: sehen
To Seek: suchen
To Sell: verkaufen
To Send: senden
Shall: sollen
Should: sollen
To Show: zeigen, präsentieren
To Shop: kaufen
To Sit: sitzen

To Sleep: schlafen
To Smile: lächeln
To Solve: lösen
To Speak: sprechen
To Start: starten
To Study: lernen

T

To Take: nehmen
To Talk: sprechen
To Teach: lehren
To Tell: sagen
To Terminate: beenden
To Thank: danken
To Think: denken
To Travel: reisen
To Trot: traben
To Try: versuchen

U

To Understand: verstehen
To Use: nutzen
To Utilize: benutzen

V

To Value: schätzen
To Visit: besuchen

W

To Wait: warten
To Walk: gehen
To Want: wollen
To Wash: waschen
To Watch: gucken
To Wear: tragen
To Wish: wünschen
To Win: gewinnen
To Work: arbeiten
To Write: schreiben

Y

To Yawn: gähnen

Z

To Zip: pfeifen

The '4' Trigger verbs

enable you to initiate any basic conversation

Practice them, especially the conjugations and the pronunciation

The following 4 "Trigger Verbs"
Enable you to initiate most conversations

Lesson No. 5	**Lesson No. 6**
To be	To have
sein (Sa-een)	haben (habehn)
Lesson No. 7	**Lesson No. 8**
To want	Can (kan)
wollen (voh-lehn)	können (Ko-eh-nen)

The 1st. Trigger Verb is "To Be"
In German, it means: sein (sein)

Let us first review the Verb "sein" (sein):

"sein" describes a quasi-permanent situation,
meaning a permanent or an almost permanent situation or condition.

<u>Examples of "SEIN" (SEIN)</u>

<u>SEIN (SEIN)</u>		**I**	**am**	**tall**	**He**	**is**	**a policeman**
Ich (Ich)	bin (bin)	Ich	bin	groß	Er	ist	ein Polizist
Du (do)	bist (bist)	**She**	**is**	**smart**	**You**	**are**	**single**
Er (ear)	ist (ist)	Sie	ist	klug	Du	bist	single
Sie (see)	ist (ist)	**They**	**are**	**fanatics**	**He**	**is**	**late**
Wir (we're)	sind (sint)	Sie	sind	fanatisch	Er	ist	spät
Ihr (ear)	seid (seid)	**It**	**is**	**late**	**She**	**is**	**beautiful**
Es (s)	ist (ist)	Es	ist	spät	Sie	ist	schön

The 1st. Trigger Verb is "To Be"
In German means: sein (sein)

Let us now review the Verb "sein" (sein)
"sein" describes a transitory situation or condition (something passing).

Examples of "SEIN" (SEIN)

SEIN/(SEIN)			I	am	angry	They	are	ready
I	Ich	bin (bin)	Ich	bin	wütend	Sie	sind	bereit
You	Du	bist (bist)	**You**	**are**	**late**	**She**	**is**	**sick**
He	Er	ist (ist)	Du	bist	spät	Sie	ist	krank
She	Sie	ist (ist)	**He**	**is**	**tired**	**You**	**are**	**out**
We	Wir	sind (sind)	Er	ist	müde	Ihr	seid	raus
They	Sie	sind (sind)	**She**	**is**	**small**	**It**	**is**	**big**
It	Es	ist (ist)	Sie	ist	klein	Es	ist	groß

Lesson 5: Part 3

The Trigger Verbs: To be =sein

Examples of verb **"sein"** (Quasi-permanent situation)	Examples without **"sein"** (temporary situation)
I am a good player Ich bin ein guter Spieler	**I am eating early each day** Ich esse jeden Tag früh
I am a great person Ich bin eine tolle Person	**I am waiting for you now** Ich warte jetzt auf dich
You are a good man Du bist ein guter Mann	**You are forgetting our date** Du vergisst unsere Verabredung
You are a disgusting person Du bist eine ekelhafte Person	**You are playing very well** Du spielst sehr gut
He is an excellent student Er ist ein ausgezeichneter Schüler.	**He is taking them to the airport** Er bringt sie zum Flughafen
He is a fantastic cook Er ist ein fantastischer Koch	**He is going to visit you this weekend** Er wird Sie dieses Wochenende besuchen
We are always here for you Wir sind immer für dich da	**She is coming home for Thanksgiving** Sie kommt zu Thanksgiving nach Hause
We are the same people Wir sind die gleichen Menschen	**We are thinking about you** Wir denken an dich
You are a winning team Ihr seid ein Gewinnerteam	**We are helping you** Wir helfen dir
You are never on time Du bist nie pünktlich	**You are happy to travel around the world** Du reist gerne um die Welt
They are the best in town Sie sind die Besten in der Stadt	**It is getting late** Es wird spät
They are the worst there is Sie sind das Schlimmste, was es gibt	**We are doing our homework** Wir machen unsere Hausaufgaben
It is better if you don't come Es ist besser, wenn du nicht kommst	**She is trying to finish her task today** Sie versucht, ihre Aufgabe heute zu beenden

Lesson 6: Part 1

The 2nd Trigger Verb is "To Have"
In German it means "haben" (haben)

Let us review first the Verb "haben" (haben) in German.
"haben" has two meanings in German:
   1) haben (haben) which describes either ownership/hold/possession or
   2) müssen (müssen) which denotes duty/responsibility

<u>Examples using haben (haben)</u>

<u>haben</u> (haben)	Besitzbeschreibend			Verantwortungsbeschreibend		
Ich habe (habe)	**I**	**have an**	**automobile**	**I**	**have**	**to go to eat**
	Ich	habe ein	Auto	Du	musst	essen gehen
Du hast (hast)	**He**	**has**	**an extended family**	**I**	**have to**	**talk with him**
Er hat (hut)	Er	hat	eine große Familie	Du	musst	mit ihm reden
Sie hat (hut)	**You**	**have**	**a problem**	**He**	**has to**	**take you home**
	Du	hast	ein Problem	Er muss	dich nach	Hause bringen
Wir haben	**She.**	**has a**	**headache**	**We**	**have**	**to see you**
Sie haben	Sie	hat	Kopfschmerzen	Wir	müssen	dich sehen
Ihr habt (habt)	**You**	**have**	**a visitor**	**He**	**has**	**to live now**
Es hat	Du	hast	einen Besucher	Er	muss	jetzt leben

The 2nd Trigger Verb is "To Have"
In German it means "haben" (haben)

Let us now review the Verb "haben" (haben) in German
The Verb "haben" in German is an auxiliary verb to Past Participle Verbs
Most Past Participle Verbs in German end in "en"

To Have

Examples using haben (haben)

Haber (ahbehr)

I	Ich **he** (eh)		
You	Du **ha** (ah)		
He	Er **ha** (ah)		
She	Sie **ha** (ah)		
We	Wir **hemos**		
They	Sie **han**		
It	Es **ha** (ah)		

I	**have**	**gotten mail today**
Ich	habe heute Post bekommen	
You	**have**	**taken a long time**
Du	hast dir lange Zeit gelassen	
She	**has**	**slept in the morning**
Sie	hat bis morgens geschlafen	
They	**have**	**studied all day**
Sie	haben den ganzen Tag gelernt	
They	**have**	**cooked all morning**
Sie	haben den ganzen Morgen gekocht	
He	**has**	**been running all afternoon**
Er	ist den ganzen Tag gejoggt	

I	**have**	**gone to eat**
Ich	bin essen gegangen	
You	**have**	**not called me**
Du	hast mich nicht angerufen	
He	**has**	**come to see me**
Er ist gekommen um mich zu sehen		
She	**has**	**taken me home**
Sie hat mich nach Hause gebracht		
I	**have**	**not gone to sleep**
Ich	bin nicht schlafen gegangen	
They have not watched TV		
Sie haben nicht Fernsehen geguckt		

Lesson 6: Part 3

Here are examples of the Verb "haben" (haben) in German,
It is used as an auxiliary verb to speak in Past Participle

To Have: haben

I have done Ich habe getan	**They have studied** Sie haben gelernt	**You have understood** Du hast verstanden
I have gotten Ich habe bekommen	**I have run** Ich bin gejoggt	**He has written** Er hat geschrieben
I have taken Ich habe genommen	**She has walked** Sie ist gegangen	**I have healed** Ich bin genesen
You have cooked Du hast gekocht	**They have called** Sie haben angerufen	**You have improved** Du hast ich verbessert
He has waited Er hat gewartet	**I have spoken** Ich habe gesprochen	**They have thought** Sie haben gedacht
She has gone Sie ist gegangen	**I have bought it** Ich habe es gekauft	**You have brought it** Du hast es gekauft
She has seen Sie hat gesehen	**She has shopped** Sie hat aufgehört	**She has bathed** Sie hat gebadet

Präsens	Müssen	Plusquamperfekt
I have a great family	**I have to see you tomorrow**	**I have received mail today**
Ich habe eine tolle Familie	Ich muss dich morgen sehen	Ich habe heute Post bekommen
I have a headache	**I have to come to see you**	**I have slept well yesterday night**
Ich habe Kopfschmerzen	Ich muss vorbeikommen und dich sehen	Ich habe gestern Nacht gut geschlafen
You have four good kids	**You have to go to eat**	**Yo have not done your work**
Du hast vier tolle Kinder	Du musst essen gehen	Du hast deine Arbeit nicht gemacht
I have a good job	**I have to meet with him today**	**I have seen her early today**
Ich habe eine gute Arbeit	Ich muss ihn heute treffen	Ich habe sie heute früh gesehen
He has problems with her	**He has to bring him the food**	**He has made a big mistake**
Er hat Probleme mit ihr	Er muss ihm das Essen bringe´n	Er hat einen großen Fehler gemacht
They have a great life	**They have to hurry up**	**They have eaten a lot today**
Sie haben ein tolles Leben	Sie müssen sich beeilen	Sie haben heute viel gegessen
You have a lot of luck	**You have to finish the project**	**We have sent her to school**
Du hast viel Glück	Du musst das Projekt beenden	Wir haben sie zur Schule geschickt
I have a rough road ahead	**We have to start moving**	**You have been absent lately**
Ich habe einen schweren Pfad vor mir	Wir müssen anfangen zund zu bewegen	Du warst in letzter Zeit abwes
You have a lot of luck	**She has to pay attention**	**She has bought new clothes**
Du hast viel Glück	Sie muss aufpassen	Sie hat neue Kleidung gekauft
She has a brand new car	**It has to be fixed**	**It has been repaired already**
Sie hat ein brandneues Auto	Es muss repariert werden	Es wurde schon repariert
It has a broken light	**I have to start all over again**	**I have been thinking about it**
Es hat ein kaputtes Licht	Ich muss von vorn beginnen	Ich habe darüber nachgedacht

**3rd . Trigger Verb "To Want" is used in German
to Express either Desire or To Give an order:**

Let us now review the Verb "wollen" (wollen) in German, it has two forms:
   1) The Verb "mögen" in German is used to express a desire or a wish
   2) The Verb "wollen" is also used to express a command, request or order.

To Want	**Examples**	
wollen (wollen)	**To express a desire**	**To give an order**
I Ich will (Ich will)	**I want to go to sleep**	**I want you to go to eat**
You Du willst (do willst)	Ich möchte schlafen gehen	Ich will, dass du essen gehst
He Er will (Er will)	**I want to learn german**	**He wants you to write to him**
She Sie will (see will)	Ich möchte deutsche lernen	Er will, dass du ihm schreibst
We wir wollen (wir wollen)	**She wants to cook for you**	**We want you to think about it**
You Ihr wollt (ear wollt)	Sie möchte für dich kochen	Wir wollen, dass du darüber nachdenkst
They Sie wollen (see wollen)	**They want to take you home**	**I want you to bring me the check**
It Es will (s will)	Sie möchte dich nach Hause bringen	Ich will, dass du mir den Check bringst

mögen (mögen)		
Desire / Wish **Begierde/Wunschz**	<u>Examples</u>	**wollen (wollen)** **Command / Order** **Anweisung/Befehl**
I want to take you to the movies Ich möchte mit dir ins Kino		**I want that you stop calling me** Ich will, dass du aufhörst mich anzurufen
I want to go shopping today after lunch Ich möchte heute nach dem Mittagessen shoppen gehen		**I want that you think about it carefully** Ich möchte, dass du gut darüber nachdenkst
You want me to bring you anything? Möchtest du, dass Ich dir etwas mitbringe?		**Do you want that we get him ready?** Willst du, dass wir ihn fertig machen?
He wants to buy a brand new pair of shoes Er möchte brandneue Schuhe kaufen		**He wants that you call him today at 2 p.m.** Er will, dass du ihn heute um 14 Uhr anrufst
She wants to try to find a new job Sie möchte versuchen einen neuen Job zu finden		**She wants me not to bother her anymore** Sie will, dass Ich sie in Ruhe lasse

The 4th Trigger Verb "Can" is used in German to express "Being Able To"
In German it means "können" (können)

können (können)	Examples:	Examples:
Ich kann (Cannes)	**I can see you later**	**He can come at noon**
Du kannst (Kunst)	Ich kann dich später sehen	Er kann um zwölf kommen
Er kann (Cannes)	**She can go to see him**	**You can do it**
Sie kann (Cannes)	Sie kann ihn sehen	Du kannst es tun
Wir können (können)	**They can take you home**	**You can come in**
Ihr könnt (könnt)	Sie können dich nach Hause bringen	Du kannst reinkommen
Sie können (können)	**He can come tomorrow**	**I can call you later**
Es kann (Cannes)	Er kann morgen kommen	Ich kann dich später anrufen

Lesson 8: Part 2

Examples of verb können

I can come to see you this weekend
Ich kann dich dieses Wochenende sehen kommen

I can call you every night at 8 p.m.
Ich kann dich jeden Abend um 8 anrufen

He can take them to the park tomorrow at 4
Er kann sie morgen um 4 mit in den Park nehmen

She can not eat chicken
Sie kann kein Hähnchen essen

We can work together to solve the problem
Wir können zusammenarbeiten um das Problem zu lösen

He can prepare for the test this week
Er kann sich für den Test diese Woche vorbereiten

You can bring them over to spend the day here
Du kannst sie vorbeibringen um den Tag hier zu verbringen

You can go to the movies with them
Du kannst mit ihnen ins Kino gehen

You can call me after lunch
Du kannst mich nach dem Mittagessen anrufen

They can complain all they want, it won't make a difference
Sie können sich beschweren so viel sie wollen, es wird keinen Unterschied machen

Ok. Let's use the Nouns, The 4 Trigger Verbs, The Magic Words and additional Infinitive Verbs to build more phrases.

I	Ich	(Ich)
You	Du	(do)
He	Er	(Er)
She	Sie	(see)
We	Wir	(Wir)
You	Ihr	(ear)
They	Sie	(see)
It	Es	(s)

The 4 Trigger Verbs

To Be	sein	(sein)
To Have	haben	(haben)
To Want	wollen	(wollen)
To Want	mögen	(mögen)
Can´	können	(können)

I have to go to call her
Ich muss sie anrufen

I want to take you to dinner
Ich möchte mit dir zu Abend essen

He can wait for you at noon
Er kann am Mittag auf dich warten

I have to go to take notes
Ich muss mir Notizen machen

I can go to see you tomorrow
Ich kann dich morgen sehen kommen

We can cook rather quickly
Wir können ziemlich schnell kochen

We have to wait for her
Wir müssen auf sie warten

I want to come to see you
Ich möchte dich sehen kommen

You can go to sleep
Du kannst schlafen gehen

She wants to cook for you
Sie möchte für dich kochen

I have to run to go to see him
Ich muss rennen um ihn zu sehen

They can come to run tonight
Sie können kommen um heut Abend zu joggen

He has to call her soon
Er muss sie bald anrufen

Additional Trigger Verbs:

To Go	**gehen**	(gehen)
To Come	**kommen**	(kommen)
To Take	**nehmen**	(nehmen)
To Buy	**kaufen**	(kaufen)
To Cook	**kochen**	(kochen)
To Wait	**warten**	(warten)
To Run	**rennen**	(rennen)
To Watch	**gucken**	(gucken)
To See	**sehen**	(sehen)
To Give	**geben**	(geben)
To Get	**bekommen**	(bekommen)
To Get	**erhalten**	(erhalten)
To Walk	**gehen**	(gehen)
To Write	**schreiben**	(schreiben)
To Read	**lesen**	(lesen)

Examples

You have to come to see her
Du musst kommen und sie sehen

You can come to watch TV later
Du kannst vorbeikommen und
später Fernsehen schauen

She wants you to call soon
Sie will dich bald anrufen

He can read pretty well
Er kann ziemlich gut lesen

They have to run today
Sie müssen heute rennen

She wants to run every morning
Sie will jeden Morgen rennen

They can take you to the airport now
Sie können dich jetzt zum Flughafen bringen

You can go to buy groceries at three
Du kannst um drei die Einkäufe erledigen

He has to get mail this week
Er muss diese Woche Post
bekommen

He has to go to get his ID
Er muss seinen Ausweis holen gehen

He has to learn to write often
Er muss lernen oft zu schreiben

Now, "Let's" build phrases with what we have learned

I have to be a good father
Ich muss ein guter Vater sein

I want to be fair
Ich will fair sein

I can be often late
Ich kann oft zu spät kommen

You have to be persistent
Ich muss hartnäckig sein

You want to be the best
Du willst der Beste sein

You can be the last to come in
Du kannst als letztes ankommen

We have to be polite
Wir müssen höflich sein

We want to be the best
Wir wollen die Besten sein

We can be of great help to you
Wir können dir von großer Hilfe sein

I have to be there on time
Ich muss pünktlich da sein

I want to be present
Ich möchte da sein

I can be there at two
Ich kann um zwei da sein

You have to be alert all the time
Du musst immer in Alarmbereitschaft sein

You want to be ahead of the curve
Du möchtest allen anderen voraus sein

You can have a lot of trouble soon
Du kannst bald eine Menge Ärger haben

We have to be waiting for him at the gate
Wir müssen am Tor auf ihn warten

He can be available later
Er kann später verfügbar sein

He has to be patient
Er muss geduldig sein

He wants to be like his father
Er will wie sein Vater sein

He can be a very good team mate
Er kann ein guter Teamspieler sein

We want to be ready for him
Wir wollen bereit für ihn sein

We can be in the losing end
Wir können am Verlieren sein

He has to be devastated
Er muss zerstört sein

He wants to be permanently on vacations
Er will dauerhaft im Urlaub sein

The Infinitive Verbs/ The Four Trigger Verbs

Ininitive Verbs		To Be	To Want	To Have	Can	Will
Nouns		sein	wollen	haben	können	werden
I	Ich	bin	will	habe	kann	werde
You	Du	bist	willst	hast	kannst	wirst
He	Er	ist	will	hat	kann	wird
She	Sie	ist	will	hat	kann	wird
We	Wir	sind	wollen	haben	können	werden
You	Ihr	seid	wollt	habt	könnt	werdet
They	Sie	sind	wollen	haben	können	werden
It	Es	ist	will	hat	kann	wird

Learning Step 8

The 4 Templates

Enable you to be conversant in:
- Gerund (action),
- Past Participle,
- Future

and

- Conditional tenses,

while using only "Infinitive Verbs"

1. Gerund (Action):

ENGLISH: To be + Verbo termina "ing"
GERMAN: Sein

How to convert an:
-       English "Infinitive Verb" into Gerund
To Walk—Kill "To"—add "ing" Walking
-       German "Infinitive Verb" declinated

Example: To Walk=gehen (Infinitive verb)

I am walking to eat
Ich gehe zum Essen

Gerund

<u>English</u> : To Be + Verb ending i n **"ing"**

<u>German</u> : Decinated infinitive verb

-In English we speak in Gerund when we refer to "Action."

-And we use the Verb "<u>To Be</u>" followed followed by a verb ending in <u>ing.</u>

-Germans use the declinated "infinitive verb" only since there is no equivalent to the Gerund form.

<u>Example:</u>

To Call: I am calling you tonight

Anrufen   Ich rufe dich heute Abend an

So, bottom line: verb endings in <u>ing</u> in English in german is a declinated verb.

How to convert an Infinitive Verb to Gerund:

<u>In English</u> we do this:

To Call----Calling (kill the "<u>To</u>" add <u>"ing"</u>)

<u>In German</u> they do this:

Anrufen --- Ich rufe an

Examples:

Gerund (action)

I am calling you, now
Ich rufe dich jetzt an

They are calling him today
Sie rufen ihn heute an

They are calling tonight
Sie rufen heute Abend an

I am studying all morning
Ich lerne den ganzen Morgen

They are studying today
Sie lernen heute

She is studying now
Sie lernt jetzt

I am waiting at the house
Ich warte am Haus

We are waiting for you
Wir warten auf dich

You are waiting in vain
Du wartest umsonst

I am writing to you every week
Ich schreibe dir jede Woche

They are writing every other week
Sie schreiben jede Woche

He is writing often
Er schreibt oft

I am trying to visit you
Ich versuche dich zu besuchen

She is trying to visit us
Sie versucht uns zu besuchen

They are trying to call
Sie versuchen anzurufen

I am learning to speak German
Ich lerne deutsch zu sprechen

She is learning about the country
Sie lernt etwas über das Land

He is learning the basic
Er lernt die Grundlagen

I am watching German TV
Ich gucke deutsches Fernsehen

You are watching her grow
Du siehst sie aufwachsen

He is watching the game
Er guckt das Spiel

Infinitive Verbs:

To Call : anrufen

To Study : lernen

To Wait : warten

To Write: schreiben

To Try: versuchen

To Learn: lernen

To Watch: gucken

2. Participle/Partizip(Past Participle)

ENGLISH: To Have + Waited (Participle Verb)
GERMAN: Haben   + gewartet

How to Convert an "Infinitive Verb" in German into a past Participle Verb:
- Use the verb "Haben" + Past Participle verb.
Examples:

Ich habe gewartet   "et" verb ending
Du hast gewartet
Er hat gewartet
Sie hat gewartet
Wir haben gewartet
Ihr habt gewartet
Sie haben gewartet
Es hat gewartet

Example: To Wait = warten
(Infinitive verb)
I have been waiting for you
Ich habe auf dich gewartet

Lesson 11: Part 1

English: To have = In German: Haben   Examples in Past participle:

+ Ich habe	To take: I have taken her home	To wait: They have been waiting for you
+ Du hast	Ich habe sie nach Hause gebracht	Sie haben auf dich gewartet
+ Er hat	To eat: He has eaten at 12	To wash: She has been washing all morning
+ Sie hat	Er hat um 12 gegessen	Sie hat den ganzen Morgen gewaschen
+ Wir haben	To learn: They have learned to read	To ask: He has been asking for you
+ Sie hat	Sie haben gelernt zu lesen	Er hat nach dir gefragt
+ ihr hat.	To talk: She has talked to him	To cook: They have been cooking today
+ Es hat.	Sie hat mit ihm geredet	Sie haben heute gekocht
	To study: We have studied	To walk: We have walked
	Wir haben gelernt	Wir sind gegangen
	To get: They have gotten no mail	To think: You have thought about it
	Sie haben keine Post bekommen	Du hast darüber nachgedacht
	To go: I have gone to see her	To come: You have been coming every year
	Ich bin gegangen um sie zu sehen	Du bist jedes Jahr gekommen
	To bring: He has brought a friend	To win: We have been winning more
	Er hat einen Freund mitgebracht	Wir haben mehr gewonnen
	To listen: She has listened to him	To buy: I have been buying lots of vitamins
	Sie hat ihm zugehört	Ich habe viele Vitamine gekauft

For a list of Past Participle Verbs see Next Page.

Lesson 11: Part 2

Past Participle (Verbs)/Partizipverben

Been *gewesen*	**Been** *gewesen*	**Arrived** *angekommen*	**Washed** *gewaschen*	**Cooled** *abgekühlt*	**Packed** *gepackt*	**Written** *geschrieben*	**Fought** *gekämpft*
Come *gekommen*	**Talked** *gesprochen*	**Calculated** *berechnet*	**Explained** *erklärt*	**Looked** *geguckt*	**Brought** *gebracht*	**Replied** *geantwortet*	**Thought** *gedacht*
Gotten *bekommen*	**Taken** *genommen*	**Seen** *gesehen*	**Repeated** *wiederholt*	**Appealed** *beschwert*	**Needed** *gebraucht*	**Heated** *aufgewärmt*	**Watched** *geguckt*
Ran *gerannt*	**Cleaned** *gereinigt*	**Called** *angerufen*	**Had** *gehabt*	**Finished** *beendet*	**Disputed** *umstritten*	**Cooked** *gekocht*	**Replied** *geantwortet*
Done *erledigt*	**Failed** *fehlgeschlagen*	**Given** *gegeben*	**Listened** *zugehört*	**Accepted** *akzeptiert*	**Built** *gebaut*	**Traveled** *gereist*	**Grabbed** *gegriffen*
Wished *gewünscht*	**Made** *gemacht*	**Walked** *gegangen*	**Bought** *gekauft*	**Asked** *gefragt*	**Wanted** *gewollt*	**Realized** *realisiert*	**Started** *gestartet*
Remembered *erinnert*	**Baked** *gebacken*	**Put** *gelegt*	**Sat** *gesessen*	**Read** *gelesen*	**Eaten** *gegessen*	**Gone** *gegangen*	**Enjoyed** *genossen*
Fried *frittiert*	**Heard** *gehört*	**Lost** *verloren*	**Liked** *gemocht*	**Stood** *gestanden*	**Bathed** *gebadet*	**Said** *gesagt*	**Searched** *gesucht*
Slept *geschlafen*	**Agreed** *zugestimmt*	**Exited** *verlassen*	**Left** *verlassen*	**Loved** *geliebt*	**Woken** *aufgewacht*	**Layed** *gelegt*	**Saddened** *traurig gemacht*
Questioned *gefragt*	**Entered** *betreten*	**Hurt** *wehgetan*	**Found** *gefunden*	**Flown** *geflohen*	**Won** *gewonnen*	**Cried** *geweint*	**Shipped** *versendet*
Ordered *bestellt*	**Boiled** *gekocht*	**Dreamed** *geträumt*	**Drank** *getrunken*	**Paid** *gezahlt*	**Swam** *geschwommen*	**Waited** *gewartet*	**Started** *gestartet*
Answered *geantwortet*	**Understood** *verstanden*	**Argued** *gestritten*	**Jumped** *gesprungen*	**Forgotten** *vergessen*	**Arrived** *angekommen*	**Dried** *getrocknet*	**Shown** *gezeigt*

3. Future/ Futur

ENGLISH: Will + Infinitive Verb.
GERMAN: Ich werde + Infinitive Verb.

I will	Ich werde
You will	Du wirst
He will	Er wird
She will	Sie wird
We will	Wir werden
You will	Ihr werdet
They will	Sie werden
It will	Es wird

Example: To go = gehen To eat = essen (Infinitive Verbs)
I will go   to eat   later
Ich werde   später   essen

Examples

ENGLISH: Will + Infinitive Verb.		**I will go to run later**	**They will go to visit you soon**
GERMAN: Ich werde + Infinitive Verb.		Ich werde später laufen	Sie werden dich bald besuchen
		You will not finish	**I will study all day**
		Du wirst nicht fertig	Ich werde den ganzen Tag lernen
		She will call you later	**They will get your food**
I will	Ich werde_____	Sie wird dich später anrufen	Sie werden dein Essen holen
You will	Du wirst_____	**You will take me home**	**He will cook for you today**
He will	Er wird_____	Du wirst mich nach Hause bringen	Er wird heute für dich kochen
She will	Sie wird_____		
			He will fly out at 3
			Er wird um 3 fliegen
We will	Wir werden_	**He will wait for you at 12**	
You will	Ihr werdet____	Er wird um 12 auf dich warten	
They will			
	Sie werden_____	**He will bring you lunch at 1**	**You will not be on time**
It will	Es wird____	Er wird dir um 1 Mittagessen bringen	Du wirst nicht pünktlich sein

4. Conditional/ Konditionelle Verben

What is a conditional verb?

Any verb that depicts a condition ; In English any verb that ends in "ould", in German any verb that ends in "te" or „est" are conditional verbs.

How to convert a German Verb into a Conditional tense Verb?

By adding the ending "de/te" or „est" to any infinitive verb (Note: as previously explained, in German all infinitive verbs end in "en"

ENGLISH: Could
           Should   + Infinitive verb
           Would

German: Infinitive Verb + "te"

Example: To go = gehen
To run = rennen
I would go to run if you would come with me
Ich würde rennen, wenn du mit mir kommen würdest

EXAMPLES:

English: Conditional	German Konditionelle Verben
Could	kann
Should	sollte
Would eat	würde essen
Would call	würde anrufen
Would wait	würde warten
Would talk	würde reden
Would study	würde lernen
Would buy	würde kaufen
Would take	würde nehmen

Infinitive V.

Can	kann
Shall	soll
To buy	kaufen
To take	nehmen
To go	gehen
To eat	essen
To call	anrufen
To wait	warten
To talk	reden
To study	lernen

He would try to finish tomorrow if he gets paid
Er wird versuchen morgen fertig zu werden, wenn er bezahlt wird
I could go to run if the weather is nice
Ich könnte laufen gehen wenn das Wetter gut ist
You should come to study only if you are ready for it
Du solltest nur zum Lernen kommen, wenn du dafür bereit bist
I would go to visit you if you would be available for me
Ich würde dich besuchen kommen, wenn du Zeit für mich hättest
We would eat at your place if you would cook for all of us
Wir würden bei dir essen, wenn du für uns alle kochen würdest
They would call you at noon if you could have an answer for them
Sie würden dich um 12 anrufen, wenn du ihnen Antworten geben kannst
I would take you to the airport if you are ready by 8
Ich würde dich zum Flughafen fahren, wenn du um 8 bereit bist
You would be very happy if you could just try to lend a hand
Du wärst glücklich, wenn du nur versuchen würdest mir zu helfen
She would wait for them at noon if they are all showing up
Sie würde um 12 auf sie warten, wenn sie alle erscheinen würden
They would prefer if you don't do anything for the moment
Sie würden es vorziehen, momentan nichts zu machen

"The Four Templates"

Through this method you'll build any phrase with an "Infinitive Verb"
Using the same verbs, l et us build some sentences using the four templates

Gerund/ Gerundio (Action)

To eat = essen; Declinate the infinitive verb

I   am   eating
Ich   esse

To walk = gehen; Declinate the infinitive verb

He is   walking
Er   geht

Participle/Partizip

To eat = essen; gegessen

I have eaten
Ich habe gegessen

To walk = gehen

He has walked
Er ist gegangen

Future/ Futur

To eat = essen; wird essen

I   will   eat
Ich werde essen
To walk = gehen

He will   walk
Er wird gehen

Conditional/Konjunktiv

To eat = essen

I   would eat
Ich würde essen
To walk = gehen

He would walk
Er würde gehen

The 11 Verbs

We revisit English grammar in order to translate properly from English to German

PAY CLOSE ATTENTION TO THESE 11 VERBS BECAUSE YOU NEED PROPER ENGLISH TO SPEAK PROPER GERMAN

To be	sein	To have	haben	Can	kann
Could	kann	Shall	muss	Should	sollte
Will	wird	Must	muss	Might	kann
May	darf	Would			

These verbs have unique features that we need to be mindful of:

1)   If any other verb follows one of these 11 verbs, there is never a "To" after it.

Examples : In English most of the times a "To" follows a 1st. verb: I have to go – I want to go – I like to go. Not on these 11 verbs: I am going – I can go – I could go – I may go – I will go.

2)   Except for the verbs To Be & To Have the infinitive form of the other 9 verbs is w/o a "To."

Example : Can, May, Shall always start w/o a "To".

3)   When asking a question with these 11 verbs, we don't use "Do" or "Did" at the beginning of the question; simply flip the verb & the noun (which is the only way Germans do it).

Example : Normally is: Do I want?-Did I have?, But with these 11 verbs we just flip":Am I?-Can I?

4)   When Negating with these 11 verbs, we don't use "Don't" or "Didn't" we simply add "not" after the verb.

Example : Normally is: I don't want – I don't have to. But with these Verbs we negate as follows: I am not coming, You can not go, You have not eaten.

5)   Except for To Be & To Have, these verbs have no conjugations.

Example : I can-He can / I may- He may / we must-they must

Questions & Negations

As you'll see both questions and negations are far easier in German than in English

Lesson 15

In German, <u>Questions are always and only formulated by flipping</u> the noun and the verb

Examples:

<u>**Du möchtest essen gehen**</u>
<u>**Möchtest du essen gehen?**</u>
(Do you want to go to eat?)

<u>**Du möchtest kommen**</u>
<u>**Möchtest du kommen?**</u>
(Do you have to come?)

<u>**Ich kann sie besuchen**</u>
<u>**Kann Ich sie besuchen?**</u>
(Can I go to visit her?)

<u>**Sie sollte mich anrufen**</u>
<u>**Soll sie mich anrufen?**</u>
(Should she call me?)

In German, Negations are <u>always and only formulated by inserting a No (Noh) right after the noun.</u>

Examples:

<u>**Du möchtest essen gehen**</u>
<u>**Du möchtest nicht essen gehen**</u>
(You do not want to go to eat)

<u>**Du möchtest kommen**</u>
<u>**Du möchtest nicht kommen?**</u>
(You don´t have to come)

<u>**Ich kann sie besuchen**</u>
<u>**Kann Ich sie nicht besuchen?**</u>
(I can not go to visit her)

<u>**Sie sollte mich anrufen**</u>
<u>**Sollte sie mich nicht anrufen?**</u>
(She should not call me)

"There is"

These two words are also expressed in German through two words:

"Es gibt"

Lesson 16

There is/ Es gibt (Es gibt)

There is: Es gibt (singular)
There are: Es gibt (plural)
There was: Es gab (singular)
There were: Es gab (plural)
There has been: Es hat gegeben
There have been: Es hat gegeben
There will be: Es wird geben
There would be: Es würde geben
There would have been: Es würde gegeben haben

"Er-Est-Y"

Learn how these endings are expressed in German

Practice them, specially the conjugations!

The Endings –er -ten

Shorter	kürzer	Shortest	am kürzesten		
Better	besser	Best	am besten		
Taller	größer	Tallest	am größten		
Faster	schneller	Fastest	am schnellsten	**Examples:**	
Quicker	schneller	Quickest	am schnellsten		
Smaller	kleiner	Smallest	am kleinsten	Shorter than	= kleiner als
Slower	langsamer	Slowest	am langsamsten	Better than	= besser als
Hotter	heißer	Hottest	am heißesten	Taller than	= größer als
Colder	kälter	Coldest	am kältesten	Faster than	= schneller als
Dumber	dümmer	Dumbest	am dümmsten		
Fewer	weniger	Fewest	am wenigsten		
Shorty	Kleiner	As___ as	so__wie		
Tardy	Später	More__than	mehr__als		
Weepy	Trauriger				

WHEN THE ENDING -ER- IS APPLIED TO AN INFINITIVE VERB
IT CONVERTS IT INTO A PERSON

To drive = fahren	Driver = Fahrer
To eat = essen	Eater = Esser
To play = spielen	Player = Spieler
To run = laufen	Runner = Läufer
To sleep = schlafen	Sleeper = Schläfer
To write = schreiben	Writer = Schreiber
To read = lesen	Reader = Leser
To pay = zahlen	Payer = Zahler
To wash = waschen	Washer = Wäscher
To speak = sprechen	Speaker = Sprecher

Learning Step 13

The Verb:

To Have

Learn the different grammar rules that apply to it

Practice them, especially the pronunciations!

El extraño caso del verbo To Have

In German there are three different uses for the verb "Haben" (To Have) :

1) **<u>Ownership or Posession.</u>** Examples: I have a headache / Ich habe Kopfschmerzen

I have a son / Ich habe einen Sohn

2)c**<u>Duty or Responsibility</u>** . Examples: I have to go / Ich muss gehen

You have to come / Du musst kommen

3) **<u>Past Participle</u>** **(Already happened)** Examples: I have done it! / Ich habe es geschafft

In german the verb **"to have"** se expresa de la siguiente manera:

haben	haben	hatte
Hold/ ownership	**Duty/ responsibility**	**(Already happened)**
I have a family	I have to go to eat	I have gone to eat early
Ich habe eine Familie	Ich muss essen gehen	Ich hatte früh essen

The Four Templates

Let's Practice

Learn different grammar rules

Practice them, especially the pronunciations!

Lesson 19

Was wird passieren?	Was passiert mit dir?	Es passiert mir
What will happen?	**What happens to you?**	**It happens to me**
Was bringst du mit?	Was würde mit dir passieren, wenn…?	Es würde mir passieren
What will you bring?	**What would happen to you if**	**It would happen to me**
Wer wird dich bringen?	Was ist dir passiert?	Es ist mir passiert
Who will bring you?	**What has happened to you?**	**It has happened to me**
Wer sammelt dich auf?	Was wird dir passieren?	Es wird mir passieren
Who will pick you up?	**What will happen to you?**	**It will happen to me**
Wer wird dich finden?	Was ist mit dir passiert?	Ès ist mir passiert
Who will find you?	**What has been happening to you?**	**It has been happening to me**
Wer wird deine Haare schneiden?	Wer wird dein Auto waschen?	Ich habe Kopfschmerzen
Who will cut your hair?	**Who will wash your car?**	**I have a headache**
Es erscheint mir zu viel	Bring mich zurück	Meine Frau bringt mich
It seems too much for me	**Bring me back**	**My wife takes me**
Kauf mir ein Paar Schuhe	Ich nehme ein Glas Wein	Du hast mich enttäuscht
Buy me a pair of shoes	**I will like a cup of wine**	**You've failed me**
Es geht mir nicht in den Kopf	Ich habe mein Auto verloren	Ich habe meine Geldbörse verloren
It does not get through my head	**I've lost my car**	**I've lost my purse**
Ich habe vergessen dich anzurufen	Ich mag sie nicht alle	Sie redet nicht mit mir
I forgot to call you	**I do not like them at all**	**She does not talk to me**

Learning Step 15

Verbs in
3rd Person

Learn the different grammar rules
that apply to it

Lesson 20: Part 1

Following is a list of verbs in 3rd Person

List of Verbs conjugated in 3rd Person

scheint	tötet	manipuliert	traumatisiert	nimmt	betrifft
Seems	**Kills**	**Manipulates**	**Traumatizes**	**Takes**	**Affects**
gebärt	beruft ein	schlägt fehl	verliert die Kontrolle	zieht an	macht
Born	**Convences**	**Fails**	**Loses Control**	**Attracts**	**Makes**
passt	verzögert	fasziniert	beendet	nimmt	schüchtert ein
Fits	**Delays**	**Fascinates**	**Finishes**	**Takes**	**Intimidates**
reicht aus	verliert	redet	kommt an	stoppt	verzaubert
Suffices	**Loses**	**Talks**	**Gets/Arrives**	**Stops**	**Enchants**
sorgt sich	verhaftet	sympathisiert	passiert	sorgt sich	schmerzt
Worries	**Detains**	**Sympathizes**	**Happens**	**Worries**	**Pains**
entspannt	sichfasziniert	fällt	begeistert	bewundert	bringt
Relaxes	**Intrigues**	**Falls**	**Enervates**	**Marvels**	**Brings**
ermüdet	verursacht	schlägt	wäscht	langweilt	irritiert
Tires	**Causes**	**Skeeds**	**Washes**	**Bores**	**Irritates**
gewinnt	weiß	vergisst	lädt ein	gewinnt	schläft
Wins	**Knows**	**Forgets**	**Invites**	**Wins**	**Sleeps**
macht glücklich	tötet	motiviert	stellt bloß	kostet	schneidet
Make Happy	**Mortifies**	**Motivates**	**Embarrasses**	**Costs**	**Cuts**
erstarrt	überrascht	verängstigt	motiviert	unterhält	quält
Stuns	**Surprises**	**Scares**	**Motivates**	**Entertains**	**Anguish**
ehrt	veralbert	illusioniert	ehrt	tötet	skatet
Honors	**Satiates**	**Illusions**	**Prides**	**Kills**	**Skates**
schockt	schockt	beeinflusst	hat	will	hasst
Shocks	**Shocks**	**Affects**	**Has**	**Want**	**Hates**

Learning Step 16

The Expression

"Ich habe gerade"

(just done/just finished/just completed "it")

English:

I have just	+ past participle verb
You have just	+ past participle verb
He has just	+ past participle verb
She has just	+ past participle verb
We have just	+ past participle verb
You have just	+ past participle verb
They have just	+ past participle verb
It has just	+ past participle verb

German:

Ich habe gerade	+ past tense verb
Du hast gerade	+ past tense verb
Er hat gerade	+ past tense verb
Sie hat gerade	+ past tense verb
Wir haben gerade	+ past tense verb
Ihr habt gerade	+ past tense verb
Sie haben gerade	+ past tense verb
Es hat gerade	+ past tense verb

Examples:

(Ich) habe gerade gegessen
I have just eaten

(Ich) bin gerade aufgewacht
I have just woken up

(Er) hat uns gerade angerufen
He has just phoned us

(Sie) sind gerade vom shoppen wiedergekommen
They have just come back from shopping

(Ihr) habt gerade zuegegeben einen Fehler gemacht zu haben
You have just committed (made) an error

(Ihr) habt gerade eure Schicht beendet
You have just finished your shift

(Wir) sind gerade gegangen
We have just left

(Sie) hat ihn gerade zur Schule gebracht
She has just taken him to school

(Ich) habe mich gerade an das Treffen erinnert
I have just remembered the appointment

(Ihr) habt gerade den Film verpasst
You have just missed the movie

Let's Practice What We have learnt

Infinitives

Example: <u>To cook</u> (Infinitive Verb) kochen   **The Four Templates**

Present	Gerund	Future	Past Participle	Conditional
I cook	I am cooking	I will cook	I have cooked	I would cook
Ich koche	Ich bin am kochen	Ich werde kochen	Ich habe gekocht	Ich würde kochen

I will be cooking		I was cooking	I have to cook	I have been cooking
Ich werde kochen		Ich kochte	Ich muss kochen	Ich hatte gekocht

I would have cooked	I did cook	
Ich würde gekocht haben	Ich habe gekocht	

Example: <u>To wait</u> (Infinitive Verb) warten   **The Four Templates**

Present	Gerund	Future	Past Participle	Conditional
I wait	I am waiting	I will wait	I have waited	I would wait
Ich warte	Ich warte	Ich werde warten	Ich habe gewartet	Ich würde warten

I will be waiting			I have to wait	I have been waiting
Ich werde warten			Ich muss warten	Ich hatte gewartet

I would have waited	
Ich würde gewartet haben	

Infinitives (Translate)

Examples: rennen (Infinitive Verb) <u>To run</u>

Present	Gerund	Future	Past Participle	Conditional
I run	I am runnning	I will run	I have run	I would run
Ich laufe	Ich laufe	Ich werde laufen	Ich lief	Ich würde laufen

I will be running	I was running	I have to run	I have been running
Ich werde laufen	Ich war laufen	Ich muss laufen	Ich war am laufen
I would have run	I ran		
Ich wäre gelaufen	Ich lief		

Examples: essen (Infinitive Verb) <u>To eat</u>

The Four Templates

Present	Gerund	Future	Past Participle	Conditional
I eat	I am eating	I will eat	I have eaten	I would eat
Ich esse	Ich esse	Ich werde essen	Ich habe gegessen	Ich würde essen

I will be eating	I was eating	I have to eat	I have been eating
Ich werde essen	Ich war essen	Ich muss essen	Ich hatte gegessen
I would have eaten	I ate		
Ich hätte gegessen	Ich aß		

Infinitives (Translate)

Examples: reden (Infinitive Verb) To talk

Present	Gerund	Future	Past Participle	Conditional
I talk	I am talking	I will talk	I have talked	I would talk
Ich rede	Ich rede	Ich werde reden	Ich habe geredet	Ich würde reden

I will be talking	I was talking	I have to talk	I have been talking
Ich werde reden	Ich habe geredet	Ich muss reden	Ich hatte geredet

I would have spoken	I spoke
Ich hätte gesprochen	Ich sprach

Exampl es: anrufen (Infinitive Verb) To call

Present	Gerund	Future	Past Participle	Conditional
I call	I am calling	I will call	I have called	I would call
Ich rufe an	Ich rufe an	Ich werde anrufen	Ich habe angerufen	Ich würde anrufen

I will be calling	I was calling	I have to call	I have been calling
Ich werde anrufen	Ich habe angerufen	Ich muss anrufen	Ich hatte angerufen

I would have called	I called
Ich hätte angerufen	Ich rief an

Infinitives (Translate)

Examples: nehmen (Infinitive Verb) <u>To take</u>   The Four Templates

Present	Gerund	Future	Past Participle	Conditional
I take	Im taking	I will take	I have taken	I would take
Ich nehme	Ich nehme	Ich werde nehmen	Ich habe genommen	Ich würde nehmen

I will be taking
Ich werde nehmen

I was taking
Ich habe genommen

I have to take
Ich muss nehmen

I have been taking
Ich hatte genommen

I would have taken
Ich hätte genommen

I took
Ich nahm

Examples: bekommen (Infinitive Verb) <u>To get</u>   The Four Templates

Present	Gerund	Future	Past Participle	Conditional
I get	I am getting	I will get	I have gotten	I would get
Ich bekomme	Ich bekomme	Ich werde bekommen	Ich habe bekommen	Ich würde bekommen

I will be getting
Ich werde bekommen

I was getting
Ich habe bekommen

I have to get
Ich muss bekommen

I have been getting
Ich hatte bekommen

I would have gotten
Ich hätte bekommen

I got
Ich bekam

Infinitives (Translate)

Examples: denken (Infinitive Verb) <u>To think</u>

The Four Templates

Present	Gerund	Future	Past Participle	Conditional
I think Ich denke	I am thinking Ich denke	I will think Ich werde denken	I have thought Ich habe gedacht	I would think Ich würde denken
I will be thinking Ich werde denken	I was thinking Ich habe gedacht	I have to think Ich muss denken	I have been thinking Ich hatte gedacht	
I would have thought Ich hätte gedacht	I thought Ich dachte			

Examples: lernen (Infinitive Verb) <u>To study</u>

The Four Templates

Present	Gerund	Future	Past Participle	Conditional
I study Ich lerne	I am studying Ich lerne	I will study Ich werde lernen	I have studied Ich habe gelernt	I would study Ich würde lernen
I will be studying Ich werde lernen	I was studying Ich war am lernen	I have to study Ich muss lernen	I have been studying Ich hatte gelernt	
I would have studied Ich hätte gelernt	I studied Ich lernte			

Infinitives (Translate)

Examples: schreiben (Infinitive Verb) <u>To write</u>

The Four Templates

Present	Gerund	Future	Past Participle	Conditional
I write	I am writing	I will write	I have written	I would write
Ich schreibe	Ich schreibe	Ich werde schreiben	Ich habe geschrieben	Ich würde schreiben

I will be writing	I was writing	I have to write	I have been writing	
Ich werde schreiben	Ich habe geschrieben	Ich muss schreiben	Ich hatte geschrieben	

I would have written	I wrote	
Ich hätte geschrieben	Ich schrieb	

Examples: lesen (Infinitive Verb) <u>To read</u>

The Four Templates

Present	Gerund	Future	Past Participle	Conditional
I read	I am reading	I will read	I have read	I would read
Ich lese	Ich lese	Ich werde lesen	Ich habe gelesen	Ich würde lesen

I will be reading	I was reading	I have to read	I have been reading	
Ich werde lesen	Ich habe gelesen	Ich muss lesen	Ich hatte gelesen	

I would have read	I read	
Ich hätte gelesen	Ich las	

Infinitives (Translate)

Ejemplos: tun (Infinitive Verb) <u>To Do</u>

The Four Templates

Present	**Gerund**	**Future**	**Past Participle**	**Conditional**
I do Ich tue	I am doing Ich tue	I will do Ich werde tun	Ich habe getan	Ich würde tun

I will be doing
Ich werde tun

I would have done
Ich hätte getan

I was doing
Ich habe getan

I did
Ich tat

I have to do
Ich muss tun

I have been doing
Ich hatte getan

Examples: arbeiten (Infinitive Verb) <u>To Work</u>

The Four Templates

Present	**Gerund**	**Future**	**Past Participle**	**Conditional**
I work Ich arbeite	I am working Ich arbeite	I will work Ich werde arbeiten	I have worked Ich habe gearbeitet	I would work Ich würde arbeiten

I will be working
Ich werde arbeiten

I would have worked
Ich hätte gearbeitet

I was working
Ich habe gearbeitet

I worked
Ich arbeitete

I have to work
Ich muss arbeiten

I have been working
Ich hatte gearbeitet

Negation

Examples: <u>To Cook</u> (Infinitive Verb) kochen

The Four Templates

Present	Gerund	Future	Past Participle	Conditional
I don't cook	I am not cooking	I won' t cook	I haven' t cooked	I wouldn' t cook
Ich koche nicht	Ich koche nicht	Ich werde nicht kochen	Ich habe nicht gekocht	Ich würde nicht kochen

I won't be cooking

Ich werde nicht kochen

I wouldn't have cooked

Ich würde nicht gekocht haben

I wasn' t cooking

Ich habe nicht gekocht

I didn' t cook

Ich kochte nicht

I don' t have to cook

Ich muss nicht kochen

I haven' t been cooking

Ich hatte nicht gekocht

Examples: <u>To Wait</u> (Infinitive Verb) warten

The Four Templates

Present	Gerund	Future	Past Participle	Conditional
I don't wait	I am not waiting	I won' t wait	I haven' t wait ed	I wouldn ' t wait
Ich warte nicht	Ich warte nicht	Ich werde nicht warten	Ich habe nicht gewartet	Ich würde nicht warten

I won' t be waiting

Ich werde nicht warten

I would not have waited

Ich hätte nicht gewartet

I wasn' t waiting

Ich habe nicht gewartet

I did not wait

Ich habe nicht gewartet

I don' t have to wait

Ich muss nicht warten

I haven' t been waiting

Ich hatte nicht gewartet

Negation (Translate)

Examples: rennen (Infinitive Verb) <u>To Run</u>

The Four Templates

Present	Gerund	Future	Past Participle	Conditional
I don't run Ich laufe nicht	I am not running Ich laufe nicht	I won' t run Ich werde nicht laufen	I haven' t run Ich bin nicht gelaufen	I wouldn't run Ich würde nicht laufen
I won' t be running Ich werde nicht laufen	I wasn't running Ich bin nicht gelaufen	I don't have to run Ich muss nicht laufen	I haven' t been running Ich bin nicht gelaifen	
I wouldn ' t have run Ich wäre nicht gelaufen	I didn't run Ich lief nicht			

E xampl es: essen (Infinitive Verb) <u>To Eat</u>

The Four Templates

Present	Gerund	Future	Past Participle	Conditional
I don't eat Ich esse nicht	I am not eating Ich esse nicht	I won' t eat Ich werde nicht essen	I haven' t eaten Ich habe nicht gegessen	I wouldn't eat Ich würde nicht essen
I wouldn't be eating Ich würde nicht essen	I wasn't eating Ich habe nicht gegessen	I don't have to eat Ich muss nicht essen	I haven't been eating Ich hatte nicht gegessen	
I wouldn ' t have eaten Ich hätte nicht gegessen	I didn't eat Ich aß nicht			

Negation (Translate)

Examples: reden (Infinitive Verb) <u>To Talk</u>

The Four Templates

Present	Gerund	Future	Past Participle	Conditional
I don't talk Ich rede nicht	I am not talking Ich rede nicht	I won' t talk Ich werde nicht reden	I haven' t spoken Ich habe nicht gesprochen	I wouldn't talk Ich würde nicht sprechen
I won't be talking Ich werde nicht reden	I wasn't talking Ich habe nicht geredet		I don't have to talk Ich muss nicht reden	I haven't been talking Ich hatte nicht geredet
I wouldn't have spoken Ich hätte nicht gesprochen	I didn't talk Ich redete nicht			

Examples: anrufen (Infinitive Verb) <u>To Call</u>

The Four Templates

Present	Gerund	Future	Past Participle	Conditional
I don't call Ich rufe nicht an	I am not calling Ich rufe nicht an	I won't call Ich werde nicht anrufen	I haven't called Ich habe nicht angerufen	I wouldn't call Ich würde nicht anrufen
I won't be calling Ich werde nicht anrufen	I wasn't calling Ich habe nicht angerufen		I don't have to call Ich muss nicht anrufen	I haven't been calling Ich hatte nicht angerufen
I wouldn't have called Ich hätte nicht angerufen	I didn't call Ich rief nicht an			

Negation (Translate)

Examples: nehmen (Infinitive Verb) To Take

The Four Templates

Present	Gerund	Future	Past Participle	Conditional
I don't take	I am not taking	I won't take	I haven't taken	I wouldn't take
Ich nehme nicht	Ich nehme nicht	Ich werde nicht nehmen	Ich habe nicht genommen	Ich würde nicht nehmen

I won't be taking	I wasn't taking		I don't have to take	I haven't been taking
Ich werde nicht nehmen	Ich habe nicht genommen		Ich muss nicht nehmen	Ich hatte nicht genommen

I wouldn't have taken	I didn't take			
Ich hätte nicht genommen	Ich nahm nicht			

Examples: bekommen (Infinitive Verb) To Get

The Four Templates

Present	Gerund	Future	Past Participle	Conditional
I don't get	I am not getting	I won't get	I haven't gotten	I wouldn't get
Ich bekomme nicht	Ich bekomme nicht	Ich werde nicht bekommen	Ich habe nicht bekommen	Ich würde nicht bekommen

I wouldn't be getting	I wasn't getting		I don't have to get	I haven't been getting
Ich würde nicht bekommen	Ich habe nicht bekommen		Ich muss nicht bekommen	Ich hatte nicht bekommen

I wouldn't have gotten	I didn't get			
Ich hätte nicht bekommen	Ich bekam nicht			

Negation (Translate)

Examples: denken (Infinitive Verb) To Think

The Four Templates

Present	Gerund	Future	Past Participle	Conditional
I don't think	I am not thinking	I wont think	I haven't thought	I wouldn't think
Ich denke nicht	Ich denke nicht	Ich werde nicht denken	Ich habe nicht gedacht	Ich würde nicht denken

I won' t be thinking		I wasn't thinking	I don't have to think	I haven't been thinking
Ich werde nicht denken		Ich habe nicht gedacht	Ich muss nicht denken	Ich hatte nicht gedacht
I wouldn't have been thinking		I didn't think		
Ich hätte nicht gedacht		Ich dachte nicht		

Examples: lernen (Infinitive Verb) To Study

The Four Templates

Present	Gerund	Future	Past Participle	Conditional
I don't study	I am not studying	I won't study	I haven't studied	I wouldn't study
Ich lerne nicht	Ich lerne nicht	Ich werde nicht lernen	Ich habe nicht gelernt	Ich würde nicht lernen

I won't be studying		I wasn't studying	I don't have to study	I haven't been studying
Ich werde nicht lernen		Ich habe nicht gelernt	Ich muss nicht lernen	Ich hatte nicht gelernt
I wouldn't have studied		I didn't study		
Ich hätte nicht gelernt		Ich lernte nicht		

Negation (Translate)

Examples: schreiben (Infinitive Verb) <u>To Write</u>

The Four Templates

Present	Gerund	Future	Past Participle	Conditional
I don't write	I am not writing	I won't write	I haven't written	I wouldn't write
Ich schreibe nicht	Ich schreibe nicht	Ich werde nicht schreiben	Ich habe nicht geschrieben	Ich würde nicht schreiben

I won't be writing	I wasn't writing		I don't have to write	I haven't been writing
Ich werde nicht schreiben	Ich habe nicht geschrieben		Ich muss nicht schreiben	Ich hatte nicht geschrieben
I wouldn't have written	I didn't write			
Ich hätte geschrieben	Ich schrieb nicht			

Exampl es: lesen (Infinitive Verb) <u>To Read</u>

The Four Templates

Present	Gerund	Future	Past Participle	Conditional
I don't read	I am not reading	I won't read	I haven't read	I wouldn't read
Ich lese nicht	Ich lese nicht	Ich werde nicht lesen	Ich habe nicht gelesen	Ich würde nicht lesen

I won't be reading	I wasn't reading		I don't have to read	I haven't been reading
Ich werde nicht lesen	Ich habe nicht gelesen		Ich muss nicht lesen	Ich hatte nicht gelesen
I wouldn't have read	I didn't read			
Ich hätte nicht gelesen	Ich las nicht			

Negation (Translate)

Examples: tun (Infinitive Verb) <u>To Do</u>   The Four Templates

Present	**Gerund**	**Future**	**Past Participle**	**Conditional**
I don't do	I am not doing	I won't do	I haven't done	I wouldn't do
Ich tue nicht	Ich tue nicht	Ich werde nicht tun	Ich habe nicht getan	Ich würde nicht tun

I won't be doing   I wasn't doing   I don't have to do   I haven't been doing
Ich werde nicht tun   Ich habe nicht getan   Ich muss nicht tun   Ich hatte nicht getan

I wouldn't have done
Ich hätte nicht getan   I didn't do
          Ich tat nicht

Examples: arbeiten (Infinitive Verb) <u>To Work</u>   The Four Templates

Present	**Gerund**	**Future**	**Past Participle**	**Conditional**
I don't work	I am not working	I won't work	I haven't worked	I wouldn't work
Ich arbeite nicht	Ich arbeite nicht	Ich werde nicht arbeiten	Ich habe nicht gearbeitet	Ich würde nicht arbeiten

I won't be working   I wasn't working   I don't have to work   I haven't been working
Ich werde nicht arbeiten   Ich habe nicht gearbeitet   Ich muss nicht arbeiten   Ich hatte nicht gearbeitet

I wouldn't have worked   I didn't work
Ich hätte nicht gearbeitet   Ich arbeitete nicht

Questions

Example: To <u>Cook</u> (Infinitive Verb) kochen

Present	**Gerund**	**Future**	**Past Participle**	**Conditional**
Do I cook?	Am I cooking?	Will I cook?	Have I cooked?	Would I cook?
Koche Ich?	Bin Ich am kochen?	Werdc Ich kochen?	Habe Ich gekocht?	Würde Ich kochen?

Will I be cooking?	Was I cooking?	Do I have to cook?	Have I been cooking?
Werde Ich kochen?	Habe Ich gekocht?	Muss Ich kochen?	Hatte Ich gekocht?
Would I have cooked?	Did I cook?		
Würde Ich gekocht haben	Habe Ich gekocht?		

Example: To <u>Wait</u> (Infinitive Verb) warten

Present	**Gerund**	**Future**	**Past Participle**	**Conditional**
Do I wait?	Am I waiting?	Will I wait?	Have I waited?	Would I wait?
Warte Ich?	Bin Ich am warten?	Werde Ich warten?	Habe Ich gewartet?	Würde Ich warten?

Will I be waiting?	Was I waiting?	Do I have to wait?	Have I been waiting?
Werde Ich warten?	Habe Ich gewartet	Muss Ich warten?	Hatte Ich gewartet?
Would I have waited?	Did I wait?		
Würde Ich gewartet haben?	Habe Ich gewartet		

Questions (Translate)

Example: laufen (Infinitive Verb) <u>To Run</u>

The Four Templates

Present	Gerund	Future	Past Participle	Conditional
Do I run?	Am I running?	Will I run?	Have I run?	Will I run?
Laufe Ich?	Laufe Ich?	Werde Ich laufen?	Bin Ich gelaufen?	Würde Ich laufen?

Will I be running?	Was I running?		Do I have to run?	Have I been running?
Werde Ich laufen?	Bin Ich gelaufen?		Muss Ich laufen?	War Ich am laufen?
Would I have run?	Did I run?			
Wäre Ich gelaufen?	Lief ich?			

Example: Comer (Infinitive Verb) <u>To eat</u>

The Four Templates

Present	Gerund	Future	Past Participle	Conditional
Do I eat?	Am I eating?	Will I eat?	Have I eaten?	Would I eat?
Esse Ich?	Esse Ich?	Werde Ich essen?	Habe Ich gegessen?	Würde Ich essen?

Will I be eating ?	Was I eating?		Do I have to eat?	Have I been eating?
Werde Ich essen?	War Ich am essen?		Muss Ich essen?	Hatte Ich gegessen?
Would I have eaten?	Did I eat?			
Hätte Ich gegessen?	Aß Ich?			

Questions (Translate)

Example: Hablar (Infinitive Verb) To talk

The Four Templates

Present	Gerund	Future	Past Participle	Conditional
Do I talk?	Am I talking?	Will I talk?	Have I talked?	Would I talk?
Rede Ich?	Rede Ich?	Werde Ich reden?	Habe Ich geredet?	Würde Ich reden?

Will I be talking?
Werde Ich reden?

Was I talking?
Habe Ich geredet?

Do I have to talk?
Muss Ich reden?

Have I been talking?
Hatte Ich geredet?

Would I have talked?
Würde Ich geredet haben?

Did I talk?
Habe Ich geredet?

Example: Llamar (Infinitive Verb) To call

The Four Templates

Present	Gerund	Future	Past Participle	Conditional
Do I call?	Am I calling?	Will I call?	Have I called?	Would I call?
Rufe Ich an?	Rufe Ich an?	Werde Ich anrufen?	Habe Ich angerufen?	Würde Ich anrufen?

Will I be calling?
Werde Ich anrufen?

Was I calling?
Habe Ich angerufen?

Did I have to call?
Musste Ich anrufen?

Have I been calling?
Hatte Ich angerufen?

Would I have called?
Hätte Ich angerufen?

Did I call?
Rief Ich an?

Questions (Translate)

Example: Llevar (Infinitive Verb) <u>To take</u>

The Four Templates

Present	Gerund	Future	Past Particip le	Conditional
Do I take?	Will I take?	Will I take?	Have I taken?	Would I take?
Nehme Ich?	Nehme Ich?	Werde Ich nehmen?	Habe Ich genommen?	Würde Ich nehmen?

Will I be taking?	Was I taking?	Do I have to take?	Have I been taking?
Werde Ich nehmen?	Habe Ich genommen?	Muss Ich nehmen?	Hatte Ich genommen?
Would I have taken?	Did I take?		
Würde Ich genommen haben?	Nahm Ich?		

Example: Recibir (Infinitive Verb) <u>To get</u>

The Four Templates

Present	Gerund	Future	Past Participle	Conditional
Do I get?	Am I getting?	Will I get?	Have I gotten?	Would I get
Bekomme Ich?	Bekomme Ich?	Werde Ich bekommen?	Habe Ich bekommen?	Würde Ich bekommen?

Have I been getting?	Was I getting?	Do I have to get?	Have I been getting?
Habe Ich bekommen?	Habe Ich bekommen?	Muss Ich bekommen?	Hatte Ich bekommen?
Would Have I gotten?	Did I receive?		
Hätte Ich bekommen?	Bekam Ich?		

Questions (Translate)

Example: Pensar (Infinitive Verb) To think

The Four Templates

Present	Gerund	Future	Past Participle	Conditional
Do I think?	Am I thinking?	Will I think?	Have I thought?	Would I think?
Denke Ich?	Denke Ich?	Werde Ich denken?	Habe Ich gedacht?	Würde Ich denken?

Will I be thinking?
Werde Ich denken?

Was I thinking?
Habe Ich gedacht?

Do I have to think?
Muss Ich denken?

Have I been thinking?
Hatte Ich gedacht?

Would I have thought?
Würde Ich gedacht haben?

Did I?
Dachte Ich?

Example: Estudiar (Infinitive Verb) To study

The Four Templates

Present	Gerund	Future	Past Participle	Conditional
Do I study?	Am I studying?	Will I study?	Have I studied?	Would I study?
Lerne Ich?	Lerne Ich?	Werde Ich lernen?	Habe Ich gelernt?	Würde Ich lernen?

Will I be studying?
Werde Ich lernen?

Was I studying?
Habe Ich gelernt?

Do I have to study?
Muss Ich lernen?

Have I been studying?
Hatte Ich gelernt?

Would have I studied?
Würde Ich gelernt haben?

Did I study?
Lernte Ich?

Questions (Translate)

Example: Escribir (Infinitive Verb) <u>To write</u>   **The Four Templates**

Present	Gerund	Future	Past Participle	Conditional
Do I write?	Am I writing?	Will I write?	Have I written?	Would I write?
Schreibe Ich?	Schreibe Ich?	Werde Ich schreiben?	Habe Ich geschrieben?	Würde Ich schreiben?

Will I be writing?   Was I writing?   Do I have to write?   Have I been writing?
Werde Ich schreiben?   Habe Ich geschrieben?   Muss Ich schreiben?   Hatte Ich geschrieben?

Would have I written?   Did I write?
Würde Ich geschrieben haben?   Schrieb Ich?

Example: Leer (Infinitive Verb) <u>To read</u>   **The Four Templates**

Present	Gerund	Future	Past Participle	Conditional
Do I read?	Am I reading?	Will I read?	Have I read?	Would I read?
Lese Ich?	Lese Ich?	Werde Ich lesen?	Habe Ich gelesen?	`Würde Ich lesen?

Will I be reading?   Was I reading?   Do I have to read?   Have I been reading?
Werde Ich lesen?   Habe Ich gelesen?   Muss Ich lesen?   Hatte Ich gelesen?

Would I have read?   Did I read?
Würde Ich gelesen haben?   Las Ich?

Questions (Translate)

Example: Hacer (Infinitive Verb) <u>To do</u>

The Four Templates

Present	Gerund	Future	Past Participle	Conditional
Do I do?	Am I doing?	Will I do?	Have I done?	Would I do?
Mache Ich?	Mache Ich?	Werde Ich tun?	Habe Ich getan?	Würde Ich tun?

Will I be doing?
Werde Ich tun?

Was I doing?
Habe Ich getan?

Do I have to do?
Muss Ich tun?

Have I been doing?
Hatte Ich getan?

Would I have done?
Hätte Ich getan?

Did I do?
Tat Ich?

Example: Trabajar (Infinitive Verb) <u>To work</u>

The Four Templates

Present	Gerund	Future	Past Participle	Conditional
Do I work?	Am I working?	Will I work?	Have I worked?	Would I work?
Arbeite Ich?	Arbeite Ich?	Werde Ich arbeiten?	Habe Ich gearbeitet?	Würde Ich arbeiten?

Will I be working?
Werde Ich arbeiten?

Was I working?
Habe Ich gearbeitet?

Do I Have to work?
Muss Ich arbeiten?

Have I been working?
Hatte Ich gearbeitet?

Would Have I worked?
Hätte Ich gearbeitet?

Did I work?
Arbeitete Ich?

German Vocabulary

German Vocabulary

A

A little: ein wenig
A: ein, einer, eine, eines
A lot: viel
About: über
Above: über
Ache: Schmerz
Address: Adresse
Airport: Flughafen
After: nach
Afternoon: Nachmittag
Afterwards: danach
Again: wieder, erneut
Ago: vor
Aid: Hilfe
Air: Luft
Airline: Fluggesellschaft
Airplane: Flugzeug
All: Alle
Almost: fast
Alone: allein
Already: schon, bereits
Also: auch
Always: immer
Amusing: amüsant
And: und
Annoy: nerven
Another: ein anderer/anderes

Anybody: irgendjemand
Anyone: irgendeiner
Apple: Apfel
April: April
Arrest: Verhaftung
Arrival: Ankunft
At (Place): bei
At (Hour): um
Automobile: Auto
Autumn: Herbst
Awful: schrecklich
August: August

B

Baggage: Gepäck
Bad: schlecht
Baked: gebacken
Bakery: Bäckerei
Bank: Bank
Barely: gerade so
Bargains: Verhandlungen
Bathroom: Badezimmer
Because: weil
Bed: Bett
Bed Cover: Bettdecke
Beef: Rindfleisch
Beer: Bier
Behind: hinter
Between: zwischen

Bicycle: Fahrrad
Black: schwarz
Blood: Blut
Blue: blau
Boat: Boot
Book: Buch
Boss: Chef
Bottle: Flasche
Box: Box
Boy: Junge
Bread: Brot
Breakdown: Zusammenbruch
Breakfast: Frühstück
British: Britisch
Brown: braun
Bulb: Glühlampe
Bull: Stier
Bus: Bus
Busy: beschäftigt
But: aber
Butter: Butter
Button: Knopf
By the way: übrigens

C

Calf: Kalb
Canteen: Kantine
Car: Auto
Careful: vorsichtig

German Vocabulary

Cart: Wagen
Caution: Vorsicht
Cents: Cent
Cereal: Cerealien
Change: Veränderung
Cheap: billig
Cheese: Käse
Cherry: Kirsche
Chest: Brust
Chicken: Hähnchen
Child: Kind
Chocolate: Schokolade
Church: Kirche
Cigarette Lighter: Feuerzeug
Clean: sauber
Clock: Uhr
Clothes: Kleidung
Class: Klasse
Close: nah
Coat: Mantel
Coal: Kohle
Coffee: Kaffee
Cold: kalt
Complete: vollständig
Concert: Konzert
Corner: Ecke
Cream: Sahne
Cup: Tasse

Curve: Kurve
Customs: Zoll

D

Daily: täglich
Dance: Tanz
Danger: Gefahr
Dark: dunkel
Day: Tag
Dead: Tod
Dear: Lieber
December: Dezember
Dentist: Zahnarzt
Department Store: Kaufhaus
Departure: Abreise
Dinner: Abendessen
Discount: Rabatt
Desert: Wüste
Despite: trotz
Dessert: Nachtisch
Detour: Umleitung
Diapers: Windeln
Dictionary: Wörterbuch
Dining room: Esszimmer
Dirty: dreckig
Dizzy: benebelt
Down: unten
Dozen: Dutzend
Dress: Kleid

Drip (Leak): Tropfen
Drugstore: Apotheke

E

Each: jede, jeder, jedes
Early: früh
Egg: Ei
Either: jede, jeder, jedes
Electricity: Elektrizität
Eleven: Elf
Embassy: Botschaft
Emergency: Notfall
Empty: leer
England: England
Entrance: Eingang
Error: Fehler
Evening: Abend
Even though: auch, wenn
Every: jede, jeder, jedes
Everybody: jeder, jede
Exchange: Austausch
Excursion: Ausflug
Excuse (me): Entschuldigung
Exit: Ausgang
Expensive: teuer
Eye: Auge
Eye Glasses: Brille

German Vocabulary

F

Fair: Messe
Family: Familie
Far: weit
Fast: schnell
Father: Vater
Faucet: Facette
Fault: Schuld
February: Februar
Fever: Fieber
Film: Film
Fine: gut
Fire: Feuer
First: zuerst, erster
Fish: Fisch
Flag: Flagge
Flight: Flug, Flucht
Fly: Fliege
Food: Essen
Foot: Fuß
For: für
Forbidden: verboten
Fork: Gabel
Forty: vierzig
Four: vier
Fourteen: vierzehn
Fourth: vierte, vierter, viertes

Free: kostenlos, frei
Fresh water: Frischwasser
Friday: Freitag
Fried: frittiert
Friend: Freund
Friendly: freundlich
From: von
Fruit: Frucht
Funny: lustig

G

Game: Spiel
Garlic: Knoblauch
Gas: Gas
Gasoline: Sprit
Generally: allgemein
Gentleman: Herr
Gift: Gabe
Girl: Mädchen
Glove: Handschuh
Good: gut
Gray: grau
Green: grün
Greetings: Grüße
Guide: Führer

H

Half: halb
Ham: Schinken

Handbag: Handtasche
Happy: fröhlich
Headache: Kopfschmerzen
Heart: Herz
Heat: Hitze
Heavy: schwer
Hello: Hallo Help: Hilfe
Here: hier
Hospital: Krankenhaus
Hot: heiß
Hour: Stunde
How: wie
How far: wie weit
How long: wie lange
How much: wie viel
Hot: heiß
Hundred: hundert, einhundert
Husband: Ehemann

I

Ice cream: Eiscreme
If: wenn
Immediately: sofort
In: in
Included: inbegriffen
Infant: Kind
Information: Information
Inside: innen
Introduce: vorstellen

J

Jam: Marmelade
January: Januar
Jewelry: Schmuck
Juice: Saft
July: July
June: Juni
Just: nur

K

Keep: halten
Key: Schlüssel
Kind: nett
Kitchen: Küche
Knife: Messer

L

Lady: Dame
Large: groß
Last: letzte, letzter, letztes
Late: spät
Lavatory: Wäscherei
Laxative: Abführmittel
Least: zuletzt
Leather: Leder
Left: links
Legal: legal
Lemon: Zitrone
Lemonade: Limonade

Less: weniger
Letter: Brief
Lettuce: Salat
List: Liste
Little: wenig
Low: niedrig
Lunch: Mittagessen

N

Nothing: nichts
Notice: Notiz
November: November
Now: jetzt
Number: Nummer

M

Machine: Maschine
Madam: Frau
Made in: Hergestellt in
Magazine: Magazin
Mail: Post
Manager: Manager
Many: viel, viele
Map: Karte
March: März
Matches: Streichhölzer
May: May
May be: vielleicht, kann sein
Meal: Mahlzeit
Men: Männer

Merely: gerade einmal
Meat: Fleisch
Menu: Menü
Message: Nachricht
Middle: Mitte
Midnight: Mitternacht
Milk: Milch Minute: Minute
Miss: Frau
Mister: Herr
Monday: Montag
Money: Geld
Money Order: Geldauftrag
Month: Monat
Morning: Morgen
Mother: Mutter
Motocycle: Motorrad
Movie: Film
Mr.: Herr
Mrs.: Frau
Much: viel, viele, vieles
Museum: Museum

N

Napkin: Serviette
Nationality: Nationalität
Naturally: natürlich
Near: nahe
Neither: weder…noch
Never: nie

German Vocabulary

Next: nächste, nächster, nächstes
Next to: neben
Night: Nacht
Nightclub: Nachtclub
Nine: neun
Nineteen: neunzehn
Ninety: neunzig
Ninth: neunte, neunter, neuntes
No: nein
Noise: Geräusch
None: kein, keine, keiner, keines
Noon: Mittag
Not: nicht

O

October: Oktober
Of course: natürlich
Office: Büro
Often: oft
Okay: in Ordnung
Omelet: Omelette
On: auf
Once: einmal
One: eins
One Hundred: einhundert
Only: nur
On sale: zu verkaufen
Open: offen
Orange: Orange

Otherwise: andernfalls
Outside: draußen
Over: über, vorbei
Overcoat: Überzug

P

Pförtner: Porter
Es kann sein: It can be Bäckerei
Windeln: Diapers
Vater: Father
für: For
Stop: Stop
anscheinend: Seemingly
scheint so: Seems like
Park: Park
Ticket: Ticket
Kartoffeln: Potatoes
Toilettenpapier: Toilet paper
Regenschirm: Umbrella
Ausweis: Passport
Payment: Zahlung
Film: Movie
klein: Small, Little
pro Tag: Per day
natürlich: Of course
Nachtisch: Dessert
Entschuldigung: Excuse me
aber: But

Pesado: Heavy
Beifahrer: Passenger

Q

Liebe, Lieber: Dear
Käse: Cheese
vielleicht: Maybe
was, das: What, that

R

Kühler: Radiator Railroad: Eisenbahn
Rain: Regeb
Raincoat: Regenjacke
Razor Blade: Rasierklinge
Ready: bereit
Receipt: Rechnung
Record: Bericht
Red: rot
Repeat: wiederholen
Reserved: reserviert
Rest Room: Badezimmer
Rice: Reis
Right: rechts, richtig
Right away: sofort
Right now: jetzt
Roast Beef: Roastbeef
Roasted: geröstet
Round Trip: Rundtrip

German Vocabulary

S

Salad: Salat
Sale: Verkauf
Salty: salzig
Saturday: Samstag
School: Schule
Seat: Sitz
Second: zweite, zweiter, zweites
See you later: bis später
September: September
Service: Service
Seven: sieben
Seventh: siebte, siebter, siebtes
Seventeen: siebzehn
Seventy: siebzig
Several: verschiedene
Shebert: Shebert
Ship: Schiff
Shopping: Shoppen
Show Me: zeig mir
Shower: Dusche
Shrimp: Garnele
Sick: krank
Sir: Herr
Six: sechs
Sixteen: sechzehn
Sixth: sechtse, sechster, sechtses
Sixty: sechzig

Slow: langsam
Small: klein
Smoker: Smoker
Snack: Snack
Soap: Seife
Soon: bald
Soup: Suppe
Somebody: jemand
Someone: einer, eine
Spoon: Löffel
Sports: Sport
Spring: Quelle
Spring (season): Frühling
Station: Bahnhof
Stewardess: Stewardess
Sticker: Sticker
Still: immernoch
Stop: Stop
Store: Laden
Strawberry: Erdbeere
Street: Straße
Subway: Ubahn
Sugar: Zucker
Suitcase: Koffer
Summer: Sommer
Sunday: Sonntag
Sure: sicher

T

Table: Tisch
Tablet: Tablet
Tailor: Schneider
Tap: Tafel
Tea: Tee
Teaspoon: Teelöffel
Telegram: Telegramm
Telephone: Telefon
Television: Fernseher
Ten: zehn
Thank you: danke
Theft: Raub
There: da
There is/are: Es gibt
Thermometer: Thermometer
Thief: Dieb
Thing: Ding
Third: dritte, dritter, drittes
Thirteen: dreizehn
Thirty: dreißig
This evening: heute Abend
Thousand: tausend
Three: drei
Through: durch
Thursday: Donnerstag
Tuesday: Dienstag
Ticket: Ticket

German Vocabulary

Time (Hour): Zeit
Timetable: Zeitplan
Tip (gratuity): Trinkgeld
To: für, an
Toast (bread): Toast
Tabacco: Tabak
Today: heute
Toilet paper: Toilettenpapier
Toilet: Toilette
Tomorrow: morgen
Tonight: heute Abend
Too (Also): auch
Too much: zu viel
Tourism: Tourismus
Tourist: Tourist
Towel: Handtuch
Track: Strecke
Traffic: Verkehr
Train: Zug
Tuesday: Dienstag
TV Set: Fernbedienung
Twelve: zwölf
Twenty: zwanzig
Twice: zweimal
Two: zwei
Two hundred: zweihundert
Typewriter: Schreibmaschine

U

Umbrella: Regenschirm
Under: unter
Underneath: unter
Understood: verstanden
United States: Vereinigte Staaten
Until: bis
Up: hoch
Urgent: dringend
Unless: es sei denn
Unwilling: nicht bereit

V

Vacant: abwesend
Valuable: wertvoll
Vanilla: Vanille
Veal: Kalbfleisch
Vegetables: Gemüse
Very: sehr
Vinegar: Essig

W

Waiter: Kellner
Waitress: Kellnerin
Waiting Room: Warteraum
Wallet: Geldbörse
Warm: warm
Watch out: pass auf
Water: Wasser
Wherever: wo auch immer

Watermelon: Wassermelone
Wednesday: Mittwoch
Week: Woche
Weekly: wöchentlich
Welcome: willkommen
Well: gut
Wet paint: nasse Farbe
What: was
When: wann, als
Whenever: wann immer
Where: wo
Where to: wohin
Which: welche, welcher, welches
Whichever: egal welche, welcher, welches
White: weiß
Who: wer
Whoever: wer auch immer
Whom: wem
Whose: wessen
Why: warum
Wide: weit
Wife: Ehefrau
Willing: bereit sein
Window: Fenster
Wine: Wein
Winter: Winter
With: mit

German Vocabulary

Woman: Frau
Women: Frauen
Word: Wort
Wristwatch: Armbanduhr

Y

Year: Jahr
Yellow: gelb
Yes: ja
Yesterday: gestern
Yet: bis jetzt
Yield: Ertrag

Z

Zipper: Reißversschluss

1- <u>Gerund:</u> Verb in Gerund required the verb "To Be" to preceed them, in German that would be the verb "sein". To practice building phrases in Gerund (Action), simply place the Verb To Be ("sein") just before the Gerund Verb using the following conjugations.

(I – Am) – Ich - bin
(You – Are) – Du – bist
(He – is) – Er – ist
(She – is) – Sie – ist
(We – Are) – Wir – sind
(You – Are) – Ihr – seid
(They – Are) – Sie – sind
(IT – is) – Es– ist

Examples:

Ich schreibe – I Am Writing
Du schreibst – You Are Waiting
Er ruft an – He is Calling
Sie kocht – She Is Cooking
Wir essen – We Are Eating
Du isst – You Are Eating
Sie kommen – They Are Coming

Notes

<u>2-Participle (Partizip):</u> Verbs in Participle require the verb "To Have" to preceed them, in German that would be the verb "haben". To practice building phrases in Gerund (Past), simply place the Verb To Have ("haben") just before the Participle Verb using the following conjugations:

(I – Am) – Ich – habe

(You – Are) – Du – hast

(He – is) – Er – hat

(She – is) – Sie – hat

(We – Are) – Wir – haben

(You – Are) – Ihr – habt

(They – Are) – Sie – haben

(IT – is) – Es – hat

Examples:

Ich habe gewartet – I have Waited

Du hast Post bekommen – You Have Gotten Mail

Sie hat gut geschlafen – She Has Slept Well

Er hat spät gegessen – He Has Eaten Late

Wir sind am Morgen gelaufen - We have run in the morning

Du bist früh zur Schule gegangen – You have gone to class early

Sie haben die Hausaufgaben zusammen gemacht – They Have done the Homework together

Examples:

I can go to eat later
Ich kann später essen gehen

I want to come to visit you next week
Ich möchte dich nächste Woche besuchen kommen

 I have to go to eat
Ich muss essen gehen